CALLED TO JACKSON, MISSISSIPPI

THE LAST
BASTION OF SEGREGATION

A HISTORICAL DOCUMENTARY

CALLED TO JACKSON, MISSISSIPPI

THE LAST BASTION OF SEGREGATION

A HISTORICAL DOCUMENTARY

BRANDON SPARKMAN

FOREWORD BY

James E. McLean, Dean,
College of Education, The University of Alabama

iUniverse, Inc.
Bloomington

Called to Jackson, Mississippi: The Last Bastion of Segregation
A Historical Documentary

iUniverse books may be ordered through booksellers or by contacting:

iUniverse
1663 Liberty Drive
Bloomington, IN 47403
www.iuniverse.com
1-800-Authors (1-800-288-4677)

ISBN: 978-1-4620-4990-5 (sc)
ISBN: 978-1-4620-4991-2 (hc)
ISBN: 978-1-4620-4992-9 (ebk)

Library of Congress Control Number: 2011915125

Printed in the United States of America

iUniverse rev. date: 09/15/2011

Contents

Foreword ix

Preface xi

Chapter One   The Call 1

Chapter Two   Reporting For Duty 12

Chapter Three   Wolves Attack 33

Chapter Four   Renewed Focus 43

Chapter Five   No Relief from Contention 49

Chapter Six   The Shock 67

Chapter Seven   *New Direction* for Jackson 72

Chapter Eight   An Era of Change 78

Chapter Nine   Battles for Control 100

Chapter Ten   Events and Incidents of Note 108

Chapter Eleven   Organizational Change 131

Chapter Twelve   Plans for Stability 152

Chapter Thirteen   Offer Too Good to Refuse 161

Epilogue 171

References 173

To

Wanda, Ricky, Rita, and Robert

who shared the hard times

Foreword

I had my internship and began my teaching career in a Southern school system during its first year of integration. While my experiences were not in Mississippi, this book not only brought back the feelings of that year, but helped me to understand that there was far more going on behind the scenes than I was ever aware. The book also brought home to me the bravery and strength of character school leaders had to have during that period if they were to be effective. The threats and problems they faced were very real! It is clear that the people like Brandon Sparkman hastened the process of integration and probably saved schools millions of dollars and possibly lives in doing so.

I recommend this book to anyone who has an interest in this period of history, especially educators and school leaders. It helps bring alive the dangers and complex decisions that had to be made. It shares the moral dilemmas of school leaders during that period. One of the most interesting aspects of the book for me was the behind the scenes political maneuverings and the inability to trust even your closet colleagues. Anyone in a high level leadership position understands how it intrudes into personal time and family life. This book demonstrates how that is magnified when involved in implementing change that is almost universally opposed in a broad spectrum of the community.

Most of the participants in this period of history have either retired or in some cases passed on. I congratulate Brandon Sparkman for sharing his knowledge in this historical documentary.

James E. McLean
Dean, College of Education
The University of Alabama

Preface

Desegregation of the races caused tension and turmoil at levels witnessed very few times throughout American history. Riots, marches, hatred, violence and murder reared their ugly heads over a span of more than 20 years of struggling to achieve racial equality. The most feared and resisted, yet relentlessly demanding, portion of the process revolved around the issue of school integration.

The period from 1954 to1974 witnessed the greatest pressure for desegregation of the public schools, as well as unremitting resistance to its implementation. During this time, one would have been hard pressed to find a daily newspaper that did not carry one or more articles addressing the issue which, ultimately, would change America forever.

The greatest trauma was experienced first in the major cities of the south, then in parts of the northeast, and mid-west. These were troubling times affecting virtually everyone. Exaggerated and explosive feelings raged out of control, often leading to conflict and violence. Administrators of school districts regularly had to face rebellious communities, hostile parents, disruptive students, defiant elected officials, unreasonable judges, and, occasionally, the Ku Klux Klan.

I encountered all of these obstacles during my efforts to ensure quality education in Jackson. There was seldom a day without problems, or even a dull moment, as I struggled trying to save the schools from complete chaos and destruction.

Within three years of leaving Jackson, I decided to write a book about my experiences in that city. I was persuaded of the importance of providing a short history representative of the struggles of school desegregation in urban, troubled, school district in hopes that this important period which revolutionized America would not be quickly or easily forgotten.

Upon leaving Jackson, I was provided copies of all local newspaper articles pertaining to the Jackson schools during my tenure there, as well as copies of certain documents and speeches marking important, or memorable, events in the district. I began reviewing these materials as well as gathering and organizing my memories of Jackson: a city with countless people whom I dearly loved, but where many of my experiences were counter to my nature.

After outlining and writing major parts of the manuscript, I put it aside, fearful of offending some with whom I had worked. After several years, I retrieved the previous work and added to it. Then years later, I did some more work, mostly polishing my previous writing. And finally, I felt that the time was right to complete and publish this historical document about Jackson.

Called to Jackson, Mississippi, the Last Bastion of Segregation accurately depicts experiences I had in Jackson, as well as some related events. Names of most characters and schools have been changed and a few slight alterations, (none of which significantly affect the historical accuracy of events) have been made to avoid offending anyone with whom I was associated.

Brandon Sparkman

Muscle Shoals, Alabama

Chapter 1

The Call

As ministers of the gospel are said to be called to their places of ministry, I was called to Jackson, Mississippi. I didn't want to go. In fact, only two weeks after my interview in Jackson, police shot two students fatally, and wounded several others during a riot at Jackson State College. Between this incident and the ensuing national publicity, Jackson was the last place in America I would have chosen to work. But it seemed I really didn't have a choice.

Two months after an initial interview with Dr. Jack Vest, Superintendent of Jackson's Public Schools (May, 1970), I received the following anonymous letter at my university office:

Sir:

> *May I suggest that, if you are smart, you will not get involved in the Jackson Public Schools. This district is in trouble deep trouble and there seems to be nothing ahead but chaos.*
>
> *May I also suggest that the superintendent is in trouble. He has lost the confidence of the teaching staff and the public. All sorts of dire and terrible things are being said throughout the community.*
>
> *If these public schools survive at all it will be a miracle that will have to begin with the community. Just now patrons are enrolling in private schools enmasse.*

> *Bystander*

That evening at home, I gathered my family around me and read the letter aloud. Our daughter, Rita, who had just completed ninth grade, was a short, talented kid who showed unusual compassion for people with problems, was generous to a fault, and always took the side of the underdog. She said, "Daddy, that superintendent's in trouble. If you can help him, we need to go to Jackson."

I looked around at my wife and our two other children. There was Robert, age 5 who had finished a great year of kindergarten. Ricky, a young man of 16, was approaching his senior year in high school. He played football, not out of love for the game, but in football-happy Alabama, if you are large with a few skills, and attending a small high school, you are expected to play football. His sport preference was baseball where he played second base on a state championship youth league team when in 10th grade. To get some money for gas, Ricky, who was not shy in the least, established a successful business going door to door to local merchants pointing out defects in appearance in their store fronts and offering to paint them. He was rather mature for his age, and had a great intellect. My wife, Wanda, a teacher, was helping support the family while I completed the doctoral program at Auburn University. Wanda was an attractive five foot eight, with brown hair, a slow southern drawl, and totally unpretentious in every situation. Among the family members, not a word was spoken, but the expression on the face of each was clear. "We need to go to Jackson."

The next day, I reluctantly arranged another appointment with Dr. Vest. But this time Wanda would be with me because a very serious decision, with great implication for each family member, was about to be finalized.

Wanda and I, in deep thought but seldom talking, traveled to Jackson to meet with the Superintendent. After introducing Wanda and exchanging pleasantries, I handed the anonymous letter to Dr. Vest, a serious, tall, trim, intent man of approximately 50, with gray around the temples, who had held high positions in the Atlanta schools prior to coming to Jackson. After reading the letter, the Superintendent responded angrily, "It's that damn White Citizens Council group. They're trying to kill the public schools."

With head cocked to the right and mouth curved slightly, I confidently replied, "I don't think that's the source. Read it again."

Dr. Vest read the letter carefully. This time, with a wrinkled forehead, a questioning intonation, and a finger drumming the desk top, said, "Sounds like someone on this staff wants my job, doesn't it?" to which I gave an affirmative nod. With an expression of annoyance, the Superintendent said, "The job of Assistant Superintendent is yours. When would you like to go to work?"

Feeling as if a bowling ball were in my stomach, I responded, "How about August 1?" And the deal was sealed with a handshake.

The Long Road to Jackson

With August 1, 1970 arriving on Saturday, I drove to Jackson the following afternoon in order to report for duty at 8:00 A.M. on Monday, August 3, the day after my 41st birthday. As I drove along, I pondered my future with the school district there. As I crossed the state line into Mississippi, I encountered a steady and ever increasing downpour of rain that made driving treacherous. "Was this an omen for my experiences in Jackson?" I wondered.

It has been said that as death closes in, often one's entire life is replayed in a matter of minutes. And so it was with me as I struggled to maintain control of my vehicle as well as my emotions.

Personal Background

I obviously, couldn't visualize my own birth but my memory got me rather close to that event. I remembered having to wear my older sister's dress while my mother washed the one or two pairs of little overalls I had. This indelible mark was made much more prominent by Uncle Rob who seemed always to sense the right moment to drop by and tease me about being a girl.

Then there was the tornado that barely missed our house as I observed the anxiety of my parents and watched through the window as trees, just across the dirt road, came tumbling down. My mother, years later, told me I couldn't possibly remember the storm because I was only two years old. But I saw it again today. I also remembered watching from the end of the field as my father, a tenant farmer, use cottonseed meal, rather than commercial fertilizer, under the cottonseed he planted. I recalled visiting the little white, two room school with my older sister one day. Asked, by the teacher, if I could spell, I gave a positive response. When asked to spell "dog," my response was, "G-O-D," and the class roared in laughter.

I recalled that a few years later I overheard neighbors talking about using hog shorts (a wheat bran byproduct from milling flour that is used for feeding hogs) instead of flour for making biscuits. Born a few months before the stock market crashed, I had observed and had been hardened by the fire of a great depression.

I recalled plowing mules, picking cotton by hand, pulling corn and fodder, and hauling hay. As soon as I could steady one end of a crosscut saw, my Dad and I cut firewood for heating and stove wood for cooking. Sometimes we also cut wood to sell. Times were hard for those who owned nothing more than a pair of mules, a little farming equipment and a crosscut saw. I could recall that when I was seven or eight years of age, my Dad would pitch me on the back of a mule and place a large bag of corn in front for me to take to the grist mill a mile and a half away. Upon arriving at the mill, Mr. Wallace, the grist mill operator and blacksmith, would take the bag of corn, help me off the mule, and crank the single cylinder diesel engine and grind the corn into meal. With the meal, warmed by the grinding process, pressing against me, I delivered the family staple.

My one great asset had been a set of loving and encouraging parents. My Dad many times reminded me that I could do anything I wanted to do if I would dedicate myself to that goal. The word "love" was seldom heard around home but it was felt always.

There were no close neighbors because this was rural, totally Caucasian, hilly, farming country. Where I grew up was a "no-named" area with a dirt road meandering in front of the tiny three-room house until WPA added some coarsely crushed limestone that made riding in a mule drawn wagon miserable.

People were uneducated. The high school graduates I knew could be counted on a three-fingered hand, but by the time I graduated, another five to eight fingers could be added. No one in this place, without a name, ever dared to dream of going to college.

As the replay of life whizzed through my mind, I that remembered my school had burned when I was in seventh grade. Since World War II was in progress and building materials and labor were extremely scarce, it was never rebuilt until I graduated. High school in the old lunchroom and the vocational building without library or science equipment, did not lend itself to quality education. But still worse, the faculty consisted of very few college graduates.

My experience as a bus driver during my last three years in high school, caused me to decided that I wanted to be a long distance truck driver. Year after year, I dreamed of this exciting career that lay ahead. But fate sometimes plays another hand. And so it was that I fell in love with a classmate who was going to college, so I was determined to go also. With no financial support available from home, My dad and I doggedly went about making plans and lining up jobs that would help pay my way through college.

But there was a problem. Intending to be a truck driver, I had not taken adequate mathematics and science courses required for most fields of study in institutions of higher learning. My only choice, without another year of high school work, would be to major in education. So, that's how I got to college and became a professional educator. Oh yes! I dated my high school sweetheart twice after enrolling in college—but at least I was there.

Three years of college cafeteria work, summer jobs and a year of picking up and delivering laundry and dry cleaning in dormitories left little time or means for social life. A few honors, including being elected Student Government President, were garnered and appreciated. As an ROTC Army Commission was received and campus life was about to fade into memory, along came Wanda and wedding bells began ringing in my head.

Army life, a baby boy (Ricky), and Korea, (with unfathomed snow in winter and rain in spring, along with tent and bunker living) seemed to further condition me even though I had already had more than a little conditioning in my first 22 years of life. But these years of seasoning provided an ingredient I sensed would be needed in Jackson.

There were three years of teaching at Phillips High, in Marion County, Alabama, a very small, rural 12-grade school. The final two years I carried additional titles of assistant principal and assistant coach. This brought no relief from teaching five different subjects daily to a total of some 240 pupils, not a good job by today's standards, but when compared with plowing mules and picking cotton, I thought it was wonderful. Spice was added with the addition of Rita, a beautiful baby girl, who came along during my second year of teaching.

Graduate school seemed like a great idea now that I had the G.I. Bill of Rights that would pay for my education. So, my family and I went on a new adventure seeking more knowledge. After a summer, an academic year, and another summer of school at the University of Alabama, I was offered, and accepted, a principalship in Tuscumbia, Alabama, a school district of 2000 students. Then after seven years as principal, I was promoted to Assistant Superintendent for Instruction, a position more comfortable to me than a pair of old shoes but more exciting than a new pair is to a child. However, the excitement was tempered to some extent by clouds on the horizon.

Meanwhile, with Rita starting to school, Wanda decided to return to college to get her degree in education. She scheduled classes that met while Ricky and Rita were in school. She was able to commute to a nearby college and still be at home with the children most of the time they were out of school. After receiving her Bachelor's degree, with the aid of some housekeeping and childcare assistance, she continued her studies while teaching in a local school district. Soon she earned a Master's degree.

I began my new duties as Assistant Superintendent for Instruction in Tuscumbia with great on-the-job excitement, but the nights were something else. Wanda and I took shifts rocking a new baby boy who awoke every hour and cried incessantly. But after a few months, Robert became a great joy and fulfillment to their lives.

The instructional leadership position offered many opportunities for exercising creativity as well as for solving problems. The year 1965, saw Congress offering unimaginable money to schools while the federal courts used their newfound powers to force integration of the races. The Superintendent in Tuscumbia, Jack Vardaman, and I pledged to each other that the schools of the district would be desegregated peacefully, and that the instructional programs would improve simultaneously.

Federal funds made it possible to bring in some of the best education minds in America as consultants, one of whom would have enormous impact upon my future. Furthermore, the extra money allowed me to visit many of the best-known and finest education programs of the time. These were difficult but exciting times, and as successes began to accumulate, I discovered a confidence building within that would allow me to move far beyond any dream I ever had during my early years on the farm.

Clouds That Wouldn't Leave

During these enjoyable years of my career, ominous clouds began to appear on the horizon and seldom totally disappeared. There was the 1954 *Brown vs. Board of Education* decision by the U.S. Supreme Court declaring separate but equal schools to be unconstitutional. The ravings by southern governors and would-be-governors, (Ross Barnett of Mississippi, George Wallace of Alabama, Lester Maddox of Georgia, and Orval Faubus of Arkansas, being the most vocal and aggressive) spewed hatred that was as contagious as smallpox and spread rapidly throughout the population. Newspapers unfailingly reported every racial incident in the south, and it seemed that Mississippi had more than its share of episodes on the printed page as well as on the TV screen.

With the help of the FBI, federalized troop, and other law enforcement agencies, James Meredith was escorted into the administrative office at the University of Mississippi to enroll as the first black student in the history of that institution. This event occurred in 1962. Then in 1963, Medgar Evers was gunned down as he returned home from attending a NAACP meeting in Jackson where he was a key leader. On Sunday night, June 21, 1964, three civil-rights workers, a local black man and two white men from north of the Mason-Dixon Line, disappeared. Their bodies were later discovered buried in an earthen damn near Philadelphia, Mississippi.

Violence against blacks included beatings and mutilation; burning of homes, schools and churches; cross burnings; and premeditated murder. Some accounts even told of white racists who kept certificates authenticating their murder of each victim. The White Knights of the Ku Klux Klan in Mississippi became the deadliest Klan organization in America. It was blamed for at least 10 killings in that state.

I was a southerner. Although my parents hated the mistreatment of blacks, they harbored the attitude of most southerners that blacks were inferior people who should remain separate from whites. Interference by the President and the courts in the southern way of life and tradition disturbed me. Then the activation of the National Guard, along with the presence of federal troops and marshals used to force integration, enraged me.

All of these tragic events weighed heavily upon my mind and emotions. At one point, I walked across the street, from the school in Tuscumbia where I served as principal, to the church where I was a member, and there asked the pastor to pray for me because, "The racial hatred that is building in me is destroying my very soul." From that day forward, I never harbored any ill feelings or resentment toward people of the black race.

Prelude to Jackson

Graduate school called once more. It was now or never. Ricky had two more years until he would enter college and Rita would follow two years later. The G.I. Bill benefits had expired due to summer school participation, and there was no way I could send two children to college and pay for graduate studies for myself. Dr. Robert Saunders, Associate Dean of Education at Auburn University, offered me an assistantship and promised to secure a teaching position for Wanda in a local school system during the anticipated two years involved in obtaining my doctorate. There could be no better deal or time, so with many tears of regret, off we went, giving up what long ago had seemed like a permanent home to the entire family.

I was assigned to the University's Desegregation Center to fulfill my promised assistantship. There I helped design desegregation plans and consulted with school systems on implementing plans, and on adjusting instructional programs to accommodate the reassignment of faculty and students.

Unbelievably, my two year stint turned out to be one year. Everything fell together so well that in the spring of 1970, I was thinking "job." I had believed that the world would be knocking at my door demanding my services, but as the curtain was rising to reveal a new "Doctor," no one seemed to be in the audience.

As I walked into the office of my Major Professor, Dr. John Walden, I was handed a sheet of paper containing a list of positions available in school administration. "See anything you like?" Dr. Walden inquired.

"No, not really," I responded. Then hesitating, I said, "I don't think I would be interested in this position in Jackson, Mississippi, but for some reason, which I can't explain, I wouldn't mind talking with the Superintendent."

"I'll let him know," said the Professor.

The next day I walked into Dr. Walden's office while he was talking on the phone. "No, this isn't Brandon's office," then hesitating, he continued, "but he just walked in. Hold on." Turning to me, he said, "This is Dr. Vest's office in Jackson. He wants to talk with you."

I took the call, and we talked about the position of Director of Personnel. Dr. Vest wanted to know if I was interested. I told him that I would like to come to Jackson and talk with him about the job. He arranged an appointment with me for the following day.

My major professor taught personnel courses (none of which I had taken), so I asked Dr. Walden if I could borrow a personnel textbook. As the professor scanned his bookcase looking for the right one he asked, "Are you planning to become a personnel specialist by tomorrow?"

"At least I should know something about the duties of a Personnel Director before my interview, I responded."

Flying to Jackson that evening, I scanned the book. Before going to bed, I went over the most pertinent parts and began to develop a concept that incorporated, at least to some extent, my love: instruction. By the time the superintendent arrived to show me around Jackson and to conduct the interview, I was very relaxed. I had a proposal to make and really had little concern about whether the Superintendent bought it. I was in a no-lose position.

New Position Born

As we rode around Jackson, Superintendent Vest told me about the position of Personnel Director, and a little about Jackson's desegregation problems. When we finally arrived at his office, he wanted my thoughts about the position. This inquiry gave me the opportunity to project a reorganization of the department and write my own job description. I explained my experience in directing staff development programs and my deep involvement in guiding instructional programs. "It appears logical," I suggested, "that staff development should be a function of the Personnel Department, including responsibility for screening applicants while keeping in mind the instructional needs of the district, and being responsible for providing and retraining staff to meet existing and emerging needs." In other words, the Personnel Department would be responsible for providing the district with an appropriate and adequately trained staff, thus allowing the Instruction Department to focus its energy on administering and supervising the critical area of instruction.

Superintendent Vest bought the idea of the expanded role of the Personnel Department, and we headed to lunch at a popular, Greek restaurant in North Jackson where the food was extraordinaire, and where plans affecting business and government were formulated. Vest indicated that he would be willing to change the title of the position to Assistant Superintendent for Personnel and Staff Development, and establish a salary in excess of $20,000 a year (more than double any salary I ever had). Additionally, he said that the district would provide moving expenses. However, he indicated that he would need to wait a few days before confirming the offer.

But then the Jackson State College shooting incident occurred on May 14, only two weeks following the interview. Riots at the black institution erupted, and police and firemen rushed to the scene to extinguish several fires set by the rioters. The National Guard was already there due to trouble that occurred the previous night. A confrontation with police resulted in the death of one Jackson State student, a high school student who had joined the rioters, and the wounding of 12 other students. From that day forward, Jackson was prominent in the national news, almost daily.

About once every two weeks Superintendent Vest would call and ask me not to take another job for a few more days. But he would always end the conversation by saying; "I've got to make a major decision before we finalize the position." I didn't understand what the Superintendent was talking about, but it was best that I didn't. Had I understood, I might have rebelled against my "call" to Jackson.

A Different Job Offer

The turmoil and largeness of the district caused me to decide that I definitely did not want the Jackson job, and calls from the Superintendent stopped coming. The Dean of the College of Education, Dr. Truman Pierce, offered me a job in Field Services, working out of the desegregation center, consulting with schools and districts of the state. Although it was more or less a holding position until a permanent job was available, I was delighted with the offer (even though the salary was much less than $20,000) and accepted it immediately. So my family and I relaxed and enjoyed the early summer months as I established positive working relationships with superintendents around the state. Then the anonymous letter arrived.

On to Jackson

The thought of that letter caused my mind to snap back to reality. With rain still falling in sheets, and even with the air conditioner on high, I was fighting the fogging windshield as I sweated profusely. "Jackson 18 miles" the road sign read. "I've got to start looking for a place to spend the night," I thought, as cars splashed by me, and I squinted, barely able to read the billboards along the interstate.

As I arrived in the city, I chose the same lodging place where I stayed when I was in Jackson for the interview: an upscale motel not far from the capitol and the Board of Education office. "It will be a long night I surmised," and it was. Trying as hard as I could, still I couldn't keep his eyes closed. It was as if they were spring loaded in the wrong direction. All kinds of scenarios relating to job, relationships, turmoil, where I would stay until the house Wanda and I purchased was ready for the family, ability to relate to and understand the work environment, family, . . . , swirled through my mind.

Chapter 2

Reporting For Duty

The following morning at 8:00 a.m., weary from lack of sleep, I met with Superintendent Vest in his office in what was a former elementary school. The building, both inside and outside, still had that 1930's elementary school appearance. However, some of the interior walls had been shifted to accommodate spaces needed for housing various offices. This building, while housing most of the central office staff, was unattractive and exuded an "unwelcome" appearance throughout. Attached to the old school was a large, rambling warehouse on the back side, adding to the eerie mystique of a facility that provided visitors with their first introduction to the Jackson public school system.

I received my assignments. As I already knew, I would serve as Assistant Superintendent for Personnel and Staff Development and administer a federal grant, in the amount of $1.3 million, which would be used primarily for staff development and to purchase instructional material and equipment. Then the Superintendent added a third assignment. "I want you to work with the court appointed Biracial Committee that is attempting to reach an agreement on provisions for a new and permanent elementary school desegregation plan."

Dr. Vest quickly reviewed the Jackson school situation, including the Biracial Committee that was just beginning its work. He discussed the constant harassment by the plaintiffs and the courts and the problems they were causing in the schools. He didn't ignore the White Citizens Council and the role it was playing in siphoning off students from the most prestigious areas of Jackson. He also touched on the staff development program that was in session even at that very moment. He suggested that

I attend that session immediately following lunch, at which time I would be introduced to many of the teachers and principals with whom I would be working.

Walking into the central office hallway and pointing, the Superintendent informed me that my office would be across the hall in Personnel, and that I would need to employ a secretary and an inservice assistant as soon as I was settled in. As we walked the hallway, the Superintendent gave a cursory overview of top staff members. Pointing to the office we were passing, he said, "You will need to reintroduce yourself to Sam Arnold, Assistant Superintendent for Administrative Services because he will handle the financial accounting, purchasing, and other related aspects of the grant.

As we talked, Dr. Vest indicated some degree of confidence in all of the Assistants Superintendents but called special attention to Jim Minor, Assistant Superintendent for Buildings and Maintenance. He described Mr. Minor as a big, stern, grumpy individual with a heart of gold, and one of the most supportive members of his staff.

Across the hall was the office of the Assistant Superintendent for Instruction, Dr. Walter Riley. Then as we neared the Superintendent's office again, Dr. Vest pointed to the office just beyond his and said, "You met Al Russell, my number one assistant, when you were here for the interview. That's his office next door."

After the tour of the central office was completed, Dr. Vest retrieved a foot-tall stack of papers and handed it to me. "Read these materials and you will have, at least, a fair understanding of where we are in regard to desegregation of the schools and how we got there," he said with a grain of sarcasm in his voice. "Court orders, news clippings—it's all there and you need to know what has gone on, what this school system has been through, and start thinking about where we need to go and how we are going to get there." Just viewing the stack caused me to break out in a cold sweat.

Having bought a house with a one-month delay of possession, I needed a place to live for the next 20 to 30 days. Dr. Vest mentioned a couple of inexpensive motels in town and suggested I check with them about temporary housing.

"I'll meet you at the cafeteria for lunch in 20 minutes, and then you can follow me to the meeting. You'll get to know some principals and teachers pretty quickly, and get a feel for what we're doing to retrain our staff."

After refreshing myself, I walked briskly to the central office cafeteria, located in the basement, and found it well arranged and attractive. There I grabbed a tray and silverware and moved down the serving line. With a healthy meal of baked chicken, mashed potatoes, green beans, baked butternut squash and apple cobbler before me, I walked to the table where Assistant Superintendent of Instruction, Walter Riley and Lawson McCreary, Director of Secondary Schools were seated. Riley, a small, gray headed, articulate, impeccably dressed, emphatic toned man, highly intelligent but defensive of his ideas and territory, who obviously postured to compensate for his diminutive size, was a take-charge kind of person. McCreary was a former junior high school principal, who, recently, had been promoted to his new position in the central office. Lawson was in his late 40's, bespectacled, bright, serious, and respectful, with unwavering loyalty to whomever he worked. His conservative credentials covered all fields.

I selected the place at the end of the table where I could talk with the administrators seated on each side. As I eased into the chair, Dr. Riley said, "I wouldn't sit there. That's Mr. Minor's seat." With that warning, I found another place near the middle of the table where my entire being was pierced by icy stares and silence.

Very soon, Dr. Vest entered with tray in hand and seated himself beside me, rescuing me from an environment of exclusion. The freezing condition during a hot, humid, summer day, along with the hurried depiction of Jackson and its proclivity for problems, made me wish I were someplace else: in a district the size I was accustomed to, and with problems that were less than overwhelming. The largeness of this district in terms of numbers, although enormous to me, was dwarfed by the dilemmas it faced. And my first meeting with the Biracial Committee was only one night away. Oh boy!

As Dr. Vest and I entered the large room filled with people. A man up front, using the chalkboard and a pointer, was explaining something to the group. As the Superintendent raised his hand, an immediate hush fell over the audience. "I have to rush to another engagement so let me interrupt long enough to introduce to you Dr. Brandon Sparkman, Assistant Superintendent for Personnel and Staff Development. Dr. Sparkman will assume responsibility for these training programs after the summer workshops are completed. You'll find him to be knowledgeable, understanding and a seasoned leader. Take him in tow now because I have to run." And that was my brief introduction to a substantial portion of the Jackson staff.

Dr. Vest had witnessed the turmoil encountered in schools of the district with white teachers facing large numbers of black students while feeling uneasy and often intimidated, even though not physically threatened. Most of the black teachers had never taught white students, and from a historic perspective were fearful of repercussions from any actions that might be confrontational in nature. The students were of different backgrounds with extreme variations in academic achievement, a situation new to both races. Obviously, the superintendent recognized the necessity of offering assistance to the staff in terms of retraining to meet the divergent needs of both students and teachers. Therefore, he had applied for federal funds for extensive staff development and retraining. This was the grant I would be overseeing.

The mostly out-of-state consultants were there to begin a long and massive effort to help struggling educators cope with the near impossible. A part of my job was to assume command of perhaps what would become the largest total teacher retraining program that had ever been implemented in America.

The presenter stepped forward and with a motion of his hand said, "Doctor, find a seat and join us." These consultants were mostly southerners, with Dr. Ron Seely, professor at a Georgia University, directing their work. Currently the presenter was attempting to form groups of twelve. He asked the participants to count off **one** through 12, then the next person would begin again with one, and each succeeding person would count aloud until 12 was reached once more. This process continued row after row until the "numbering" reached the row where I was seated. The person immediately to my left loudly said, "12. And just as loudly as the preceding person, I shouted, "13."

The room rocked with laughter. The color of my face and neck, apparently, portrayed my humiliation, which further enhanced the humor of the moment. "Damn, what a time to screw up," I thought. The first thing the group learned about the new person who had been brought to Jackson to be in charge of their training was that I was not perfect—and maybe this was good.

As soon as the meeting ended, I drove back to the central office and headed straight for the 9 x 10 foot room that was my assigned domain. The space provided no privacy since there were windows on the two sides facing hallways and on a third side facing the personnel office. At least it was clean.

I found a modest desk, file cabinet, two padded straight chairs, and a telephone. Someone had placed a legal pad, a pen, two pencils and a stapler on the desk. That was it. There was little there that made me feel like this was a friendly, usable office like the ones I had been accustomed to having. The other offices were closed because of the lateness of the day, so I dejectedly left the building.

Roughing It

Trudging through the rain, I set out to find a place to serve as a home-away-from-home. My new home was a dingy, minimally acceptable, room with two sagging double beds. It wasn't great and neither was its location, but the price was attractive. Virtually hidden behind other buildings, it gave the appearance of a hideaway for illicit business. It was a cheap room in a cheap environment, much as one would expect of a motel where many of its rooms had multiple daily rentals. I couldn't afford even minimal comfort so I settled for this shabby inn for the month of August.

The next morning when I awoke, I could hear the rain. I wondered if it rained every day in Mississippi. For three days it had rained off and on, and for the next 17 days it never missed a beat. It was hot, wet, humid, and just downright uncomfortable. The weather, no doubt, was taking its lead from my personal feeling: no family to comfort and share, a crummy motel room for a home, hamburgers and candy bars for food, and an environment of turmoil and hostility. Other than Superintendent Vest, I was the only outsider among the central office staff, and soon I would find that I was neither wanted nor trusted by a large segment of my counterparts.

Quick Introduction

Tuesday morning, I found my desk and was greeted warmly by the Assistant Director of Personnel. She showed me around the personnel office and introduced me to the staff. Sandra Wells, a petite, single woman in her mid-thirties, proudly educated at Milsaps College in Jackson, with neat appearance and pleasant expressions, wearing a meticulously starched and ironed skirt and a high-necked blouse, Sandra exhibited an air of professionalism. She appeared to be more knowledgeable about personnel functions than I ever wanted, or was likely, to be. The way she moved, talked, and carried herself told me that she was efficient, mannerly, and in control. She spent more than an hour explaining the duties that had been performed by the previous Director of Personnel and in going over procedures, forms and files. She pointed out that she had a seasoned staff that could handle most things until I became familiar with the operation. The most pressing thing she said was employing two assistant principals. These were positions on which she wanted my input before making an offer. She had lined up interviews with two prime candidates for the next day and wanted me to participate.

As we walked into the office assigned to me, Sandra told me that I would need to get with Jim Minor in order to get my office properly equipped. When I asked about office space for a secretary, she said that Mr. Minor also assigns offices, and that I would have to consult with him. She apologized that the office was so poorly equipped.

"In regard to a secretary for you, I have one who is excellent, and I would be willing for you to take her, if you like," Sandra suggested. I indicated that I would think about that, and maybe I could talk with her in a day or two. Just then, a staff member came to the door and reported that the Superintendent would like to see me.

The next couple of hours were spent with Superintendent Vest, who with head tilted slightly, facial muscles tightly drawn, and a slight twitch of the right eye, again explained the basic function of the Biracial Committee. This group was to resolve issues interfering with the formation of a unitary school system. Additionally, they were to agree on an elementary desegregation plan acceptable to both parties and to the court. Dr. Vest stated that good people were on the committee. "You've had some experience in helping design desegregation plans. I think you can help the committee to coalesce while serving as an observer: not as a member."

Back in my office, I met with Sandra, this time to draw up notices of vacancies for the positions of Secretary and Inservice Assistant. Further, job descriptions were designed for the new positions. The job vacancy notices would have to be posted five working days prior to interviews. Sandra left my office then returned shortly to place a large stack of papers on my desk for signature. I browsed through the stack, and then one by one I examined the papers and placed my autograph on each. My thoughts were, "We're going to change some procedures around here. I'm not spending my life writing my name."

"Maybe time for a quick bite," I thought as I left my office. "And where am I going to find that," I said to myself—totally unfamiliar with the "big city". This was my first experience residing in a metropolitan area.

Trying to swallow my last bite of hamburger, but still hanging on to my drink, I arrived at the boardroom, a space of about 30x 60 feet, with armless chairs in rows occupying approximately two-thirds of the area near the room's rear entrance. An extensive, polished board table, surrounded by plush leather-covered armchairs occupied most of the remaining space in this room.

There I met with the 12 member Biracial Committee composed of an equal number of black and white representatives. I hadn't met any of the members previously, so I knew nothing about them at the time; however, as I discovered later, they were some of Jackson's most influential leaders. They were not at the peak of the power structure, with one exception, but just beneath. I seated myself on the front row in one of the armless chairs, and later discovered that I was the only non-member in attendance.

As the meeting proceeded, it appeared to me that these people were more determined to disagree than to resolve differences. When a white person raised a point, the blacks, using Justin Cohen as spokesman most of the time, immediately attacked ideas, or rejected them outright. Mr. Cohen, a New York Jew married to a black woman, was a NAACP Legal Defense Fund attorney who had moved to Jackson, and had filed numerous suits against Mississippi school districts and against Jackson. He was not only the spokesperson for black members of this committe, and was at the peak of the power structure among blacks and ultra-liberal whites in Jackson, and was, without a doubt, the most despised man in the state of Mississippi. The same approach was taken by whites much of the time when blacks presented an idea.

Disagreements went back and forth all evening. The whites were attempting to be, as I viewed it, reasonable, yet guarded in their proposals, while the black side appeared to push beyond that which could reasonably be accomplished. Perhaps having won 11 Fifth Circuit Court of Appeals cases against the Jackson Schools, they felt that they didn't have to yield to anyone on anything. Whatever it was that was taking place, the whole thing was very discouraging to me, and I was glad when the meeting ended, even without any sign of progress having been made.

The remainder of the week was spent attending staff development meetings, talking with principals and central office staff, and trying to persuade Jim Minor to properly furnish my office and get me a private line for my telephone. The one line for the entire personnel office meant that I rarely had access for making or receiving calls.

Oh yes, there was the staff meeting on Wednesday called by Superintendent Vest. As I walked into the Board room, six staff members were already seated around the long board table. I noticed that the last chair on my left on the front side of the table was vacant. I slowly sank into the rather plush seat. Immediately, Al Russell said, "Sparkman, if I were you, I'd move to another chair. That's Jim's seat."

Slowly rising, I somewhat sarcastically asked, "Is there an unclaimed seat around the table?"

"Aw, just any of the others will do," Al responded. Al Russell, in his middle 60's, was the Assistant Superintendent for Administration and was second in command. A seasoned administrator, he was serious but easy going, respectful, and a man of unblemished integrity. Although having served in his position for many years, he still referred most difficult questions to the Superintendent. Some of the staff felt that he was just serving out his time with little, other than retirement, on his mind. But perhaps his lack of drive could more correctly be attributed to the unmanageable and unsolvable problems that he faced on a daily basis with a blurred view of the end of the tunnel, at best,—or maybe even the tunnel itself.

I looked forward to Friday afternoon in much the same way a kid looks forward to visiting the local ice cream shop. I had spent one lonely week, and my burning desire to see Wanda, Ricky, Rita, and Robert was causing time to virtually stand still.

The Second Week

Arriving back in Jackson late Sunday night, I tossed and turned, sleeping uneasily until morning light told me that I should go ahead and get up even though my clock had not sounded. I took a quick shower, shaved and climbed into my clothes. A stop at McDonald's for some warm food and hot coffee aroused in me an "I think I can" feeling for the day, even though the weather had not flinched.

I had hardly seated myself in my office chair when Dr. Vest walked in, hung a cheek on a corner of my desk, and broke the news. "Brandon, I'm sorry, but the doctor is putting me in the hospital this morning. I don't know how long I'll be there, but just hang on and do the best you can until I get back." And he dashed out.

I spent time with Jim Minor, a tall (maybe 6' 4"), overweight, 60ish appearing hulk of a man, somber, grouchy and demanding. Minor carried significant weight, other than his own, in the organization. As I had already observed, few, if any who knew him, dared to cross him. He authored the manual on intimidation.

After outlining my needs for office furniture and equipment, I reminded Jim that I would be hiring a secretary and an inservice assistant, both of whom would need office space.

"We're out of space here, and as you will learn from Sam, there's little or no money for making unbudgeted purchases. We'll do the best we can, but there will be some constraints that you will have to understand."

Conflict with Cohen

The next evening, another meeting of the Biracial Committee was held. This meeting was a reprint of the previous one. Several times, proposals made by Mr. Cohen would have, if adopted, totally destroyed the Jackson schools, yet he refused to move from his position. Counter proposals were immediately rejected. And so it went for the first hour.

A break was taken and as Mr. Cohen walked outside the building to smoke, I followed him. After we had talked briefly, I pointed out to him how his last proposal would be detrimental to the education process for all children. Cohen's response was, "I don't give a damn about children and education. My only interest is in mixing black and white bodies."

Taken aback momentarily, I suddenly countered, "Then I have absolutely no respect for you. Anyone who cares nothing about the welfare of children and their education deserves no respect because they have no respect for others. You're unworthy to represent black people." With that, I turned quickly and walked back into the building. I was so angry that I remembered little that happened during the remainder of that session.

View of Jackson's Past

The stack of documents handed to me by Jack Vest had remained in the motel dresser drawer, virtually untouched. However, having experienced two Biracial Committee meetings, I determined that time for procrastination was past, so I dug into the material.

I found that Dr. Harry Prince had served as Superintendent of the Jackson schools for more than three decades prior to his retirement and the employment of Dr. Jack Vest. Dr. Prince, a tall, slim, fast talking, self-confident, gregarious individual had developed one of the finest school systems in the state, and some would even say the nation, that is, if one considered white students only. He quickly gained the respect of both community and staff and developed a loyalty among both that was difficult for most to transfer and impossible for many to do so.

The "Colored Schools" were run largely by a black director, the latest one being Mr. Johnny Wise, whose background was in music in another school district. He was lured to Jackson by Dr. Prince who had detected Johnny's intellect, glowing personality and leadership ability. He was a person of average size and build, in his early 60's, personable, friendly, and careful not to appear pushy or too knowledgeable while around white people. Obviously, he had learned to assume an acceptable behavior for every situation faced. Whether you liked black people or not, you could not easily dislike Johnny Wise.

Dr. Prince designed a curriculum and instructional program, particularly effective in the white schools, which were adhered to strictly, leaving little room for adjusting to fit the needs of those who did not parallel the norm of the day. The curriculum for "Colored" Schools was the same as for white schools but enforcement basically was left to the discretion of the Director. There was little planning or coordination of that which was taught until shortly before the retirement of Dr. Prince. Mr. Wise began correcting that deficiency after assuming the office of

Assistant Director of Colored Schools in the early 1960's and proceeded more aggressively upon being appointed Director. But the years of neglect had created a quality chasm between the level of education for blacks and whites that would take years and untold anguish to bridge.

Legal Battles Begin

The year was 1948 when the Jackson Board received a petition from one of its black teachers asking it to discontinue the policy and custom of discrimination in salaries of Negro teachers and principals based on race and color. An inadequate Board response caused the teacher to take the matter all the way to the U.S Supreme Court, which rejected the case.

Brown vs. Board of Education in 1954 laid the groundwork for numerous petitions, injunctions, processes and suits which consumed so much time and money that attention to instruction in the Jackson schools was moved to the back burner.

The first demand by the NAACP in Jackson occurred when the district closed two black schools and directed that these students attend a school near Tougaloo in north Jackson. Just before court action, the Board agreed to contract with a commercial bus line to provide transportation for children living two or more miles from the school.

State Power Structure Convenes

As the heat of black vs. white issues went from smoke to visible flames, behind the scene, plans were being formulated. A meeting of the rich and powerful was held in the corporate boardroom of a respected Jackson company. With the power structure of the state of Mississippi present, a vow was made that integration would not be permitted in the state. Each participant pledged his support and money to that end. And so, the Ku Klux Klan was assured of the financial means needed, not just to deter, but to destroy any movement that threatened their southern way of life.

Battle Lines Drawn

In July 1962, the Superintendent and the Board received a petition demanding that the Jackson Board reorganize the schools on a non-discriminatory basis as required by the *Brown vs. Board of Education* decision. A young black man, Medgar Evers, active in the Jackson Branch of NAACP, signed the document, along with several others. Shortly thereafter, a suit was filed in federal court asking that the Jackson schools be desegregated. Now, the legal assault against the Jackson Board was gaining momentum. Sadly, Evers never knew the outcome of the suit because a few months later he was fatally shot on his way home from a NAACP meeting. This callous act only further inflamed the black community and the nation.

Also in 1962, with the aid of federal marshals and the military, the first black, James Meredith, enrolled at the University of Mississippi. Concurrent with these actions, the Ku Klux Klan, with unlimited financial support from the power structure of the state, was frantically trying to stop a movement that was somewhat akin to attempting to repair a collapsed dam across a major tributary during a flood. Threats and violence were omnipresent.

Mississippi was the last state to begin integration of its schools, but in 1964 Jackson bowed to court orders and pressure and admitted a few black first graders into white schools. Additionally, the Board accepted a "one-grade-at-a-time" desegregation plan ordered by the court.

The White Citizens Council stepped up its pace in offering an all-white school choice for parents. As integration increased, so did the number of classrooms in the Council Schools. The so-called "Segregation Academies," along with newly formed parochial schools, eventually siphoned off almost half of the white students from the Jackson schools.

Aggravated Appellate Court

One court order could not be implemented before another was handed down. Nevertheless, the Jackson Board, with its attorneys, found ways to delay responding to and implementing orders by foot dragging and appealing orders to higher courts as long as possible. Superintendent Prince, shocked and frustrated by the speed things were moving, never attempted to accept the inevitable. Perhaps he wanted to take the initiative and end the fighting, but he had little choice. He would lose all of his close friends and be considered a traitor to the community. But those close to him could see the toll the fights were taking on him.

The Federal District Judges were sympathetic to the cause of segregation and consistently ruled in favor of the Board. Then upon appeal by the plaintiff to the Fifth Circuit Court of Appeals in New Orleans, local court decisions were overturned. And each time an order was reversed, the school district dug in a little deeper until a new suit with even greater implications was filed.

Eleven suits were filed against the Jackson Board and 11 times the plaintiffs won. Court orders that forced integration of schools located in ghetto areas found little success. White parents would not send their children into these areas, and the fact that white students did not attend was interpreted by the courts to mean that the ordered plan was ineffective. Then a new order expanding the zone further into the white community was issued, hoping to fully integrate the school district. The fact was that these orders were driving white students out of public education by the thousands thus eventually causing further, and perhaps, permanent segregation. While overly aggressive and determined Fifth Circuit Appellate judges might be blamed for over zealousness, surely much of their attitude could be attributed to the dogged resistance to the orders by elected state officials and local school authorities.

New York Comes to Jackson

The New York office of NAACP Legal Defense Fund decided to take charge of the cases in Mississippi, so it sent a cadre of attorneys to Jackson. They began to push for further and more rapid changes in the Jackson schools. Each case was heard, appealed, heard again, but always ruled in favor of the plaintiff. The School Board and administrative staff felt as if they were in the middle of a tornado, trying their best to hang on but losing grip by the minute.

Change of Guard

By September of 1967, all grades in Jackson's Schools had been integrated, but the fight had only begun. More orders heaped on more orders were an endless and vicious cycle causing rapid deterioration of educational quality. Not only were the courts a major factor affecting the wellbeing of Dr. Prince, but also groups of NAACP members regularly visited the central office building and his office making demands and harassing him. He was pressured on every side; not only those who sought change in the racial makeup of the school district, but also by his many friends and supporters who urged him not to relent. Superintendent Prince, already past retirement age, determined that for his own health and sanity he must step down.

An Outsider Takes Over

Faced with finding a Superintendent to replace Dr. Prince, the Board of Education employed a team to search the nation for the best available. In mid-summer 1969, Dr. Jack Vest arrived from Atlanta, Georgia to take up the fight where Dr. Prince had left off. Having experience in the Atlanta schools, a much larger urban district, he had faced similar problems, but of much less severity. The new Superintendent, in his visit, interview, and investigation of Jackson, had greatly misjudged the jungle he was about to enter.

The Board, city officials and the business people received Dr. Vest with a degree of enthusiasm and support, whereas, the community was reluctant to trust him. Dr. Prince had never let them down, and the people wondered how the new out-of-state educational leader was going to handle the brutal forces attacking their way of life

Every time the plaintiffs won a court battle, Superintendent Vest was blamed. He was an outsider, and people questioned his understanding and commitment to Mississippi values.

Justin Cohen was assigned to the Jackson office of NAACP Legal Defense Fund that same year. Mr. Cohen moved to Jackson and immediately began pursuing many suits against school districts throughout the state as well as the Jackson School District. He promptly became the most hated man in Mississippi. Not only did he have great success in court, but also he quickly established himself as spokesman for the blacks and ultra-liberal whites of Jackson, rapidly reaching the peak of the power structure of this group.

Late in 1969, a Fifth Circuit Court order was handed down that required the district to totally desegregate its teaching staff immediately. But within two weeks of the School Board announcement that faculties were being reshuffled, a new order replacing the previous one was received requiring students as well as staff to be reassigned. That order so angered the white community that Superintendent Vest's chance of being accepted in Jackson was totally destroyed. He was perceived as a weak-kneed leader who had let the public schools be damaged beyond repair.

The schools were closed for two weeks near the end of January 1970 while student attendance lines were redrawn and teachers were reassigned by lottery. The black/white ratio of teachers in each school had to reflect the black/white ratio of students throughout the school district. When schools reopened in early February, more than 4,000 white students failed to return to the Jackson Public Schools.

Unmanageable Change

A report of the *Education Taskforce* of the Jackson Chamber of Commerce provides a rather succinct history of the raging change that occurred in the Jackson schools in roughly one year.

In September of 1969, one year ago, schools of this district opened under what was basically a "freedom of choice" plan. Enrollment showed 18,227 blacks and 20,966 whites. Today, one year and three court ordered plans later, enrollment is 18,396 black and 12,095 white, a 42.2 percent decrease in the number of whites. The first court order last fall ordered desegregation of staff at the beginning of the second semester. On appeal by the NAACP Legal Defense Fund, counsel for the plaintiff, complete desegregation of pupils and staff was ordered at the beginning of the second semester. The District Judge ordered into effect an HEW plan for elementary schools and a plan of his own devising for secondary schools. Plaintiffs appealed this order as to the secondary plan only. In May the Fifth Circuit Court of Appeals acted on this appeal, ordering into effect a HEW plan for secondary schools. Although there had been no appeal, the Fifth Circuit ordered the District Court to prepare a new elementary plan and ordered the appointment of a Bi-Racial Committee to help devise this plan. The Bi-Racial Committee did devise a plan and, after hearings, this plan was ordered into effect for September. Plaintiffs appealed this order and in their brief made this statement: "The district court's controlling responsibility is to evaluate that plan, not in terms of its educational soundness, but in terms of its ability to achieve integration."

In August, acting on this appeal, the Fifth Circuit ordered into effect a plan which basically consisted of the pairing and grouping of approximately half the elementary schools. The court stated that this was to be temporary and the District Court was ordered to hold hearings and to prepare a new elementary plan for the second semester, making the fourth disruption in four semesters. The traditional six-grade structure for elementary schools has been destroyed and we now have seven different grade-structured types of elementary schools. The traditional 3-3 secondary structure has been destroyed in favor of a 2-1-1-2 structure.

Under court plans presently in effect, 95% of the children in this district will attend six different schools from the first to the twelfth grade. On one extreme case, a small group of children will go to seven schools in twelve years. Or to look at it another way, it is possible for a family with seven children to have them in seven different schools. [1]

From the beginning of serious integration of the Jackson Schools until the fall of 1970, more than 10,000 white students withdrew, changing from a white/black ratio of roughly 60/40 to a black majority in the district.

The Klan was unhappy with the presence of Dr. Vest, so he and his family were constantly harassed and threatened. He had an unlisted phone number installed at home because of the threats and vulgarity his family regularly heard. And from time to time, threats were perceived to be so serious that Dr. Vest had police escorts to and from work.

New court orders kept coming so fast that one could not be implemented before another arrived, including changes in traditional grade structures. The white community was totally disgusted with the trauma forced upon their children, but the courts were not happy either. So they kept issuing new orders including an order for a temporary arrangement until still another plan could be agreed upon. Therefore, an order was issued requiring the Jackson School Board, the NAACP, the Department of Health Education and Welfare (HEW) and a Biracial Committee, which it appointed, to submit a new elementary desegregation plan for court approval that was mutually acceptable by June 22, 1971.

---

[1]   Jackson Chamber of Commerce, *"Education Taskforce Report"*, Unpublished Report (September, 1970)

Power Structure Reconvenes

The same corporate boardroom was the site of the second meeting of the state's power structure. These powerbrokers were ready to change sides. Obviously, this group with great prestige, money and power could not stop the inevitable. The image of the state had already been damaged severely and these businessmen could visualize their accumulated and anticipated fortunes going down the drain. Company after company seeking to locate a new plant passed on Mississippi. Boycotts were having adverse effect on the state economy and intrastate sales had decreased at an alarming rate. The image of the state was taking a terrible beating. But even worse, the FBI had "broken the back" of the Klan. The consensus was that support must be withdrawn from the Klan and shifted to peaceful integration of the races; otherwise their businesses would deteriorate even further. Not a single attitude had changed. Fact was that the men saw the necessity of swimming with the tide even though they despised the water.

Back at Work

"Would you like to interview Sue Ann this morning?" Sandra asked regarding her secretary.

"Sure," I replied. Then, Sue Ann, a woman in her late 30's, walked in wearing a dress of bland colors. She exhibited little enthusiasm or excitement outwardly; and when asked about her typing skills, she admitted she could type. Pressed about her shorthand ability, she said she could do fairly well. Obviously, if Sue Ann were proficient in secretarial skills, she intended to keep it a secret.

My conclusion: Sandra had a problem on her hand that she wanted to pass on to me. I began looking elsewhere.

Lisa Smith, a cute young thing just out of high school, was interviewed next. Looking sharp with eyes sparkling, she had a positive answer ready for every question. Great typist, master of shorthand, excellent record in grammar and writing skills were her avowed attributes. So, I hired her.

Another Committee Assignment

"I have another important assignment for you," Dr. Vest ventured during the second week of my tenure. Then he spent some time talking about T.E.M.P.O., a nationally respected consulting firm that had been employed to make a thorough study of every function of the district and to make recommendations for change. Vest needed an outside and objective view of the district accompanied by suggestions for improving it quickly. Then he delved more deeply into the court orders and the fact that the district was facing a new elementary order that would replace the current one. Since the court was expected to impose a totally unmanageable plan designed by the Civil Rights Division of Health, Education and Welfare (HEW), unless the Board of Education and the Black leaders arrived at a mutually acceptable plan, it was imperative that the Board beat the court deadline. Therefore, with the Board's knowledge, Dr. Vest was temporarily diverting the original assignment of this consulting firm by asking them, along with some key business and industrial leaders, and me, to design a desegregation plan that the district could live with and the black leadership and the court would accept. So now, I was working with two committees with the same objective.

Office Problems

Jim Minor was finally persuaded to furnish a small used desk and typewriter for my new secretary. The desk was squeezed into a corner of my office where now I would have to work, talk with people, and do interviews with my young secretary present, or else stop her work and send her outside my office. After a couple days of this arrangement, I told Sandra that she would need to rearrange the Personnel office reception area to make room for Lisa and her desk.

I learned quickly that my greatest asset was not my ability to interview and chose the best person for a secretarial position. I dictated a letter to Lisa slowly and hesitatingly because she was constantly asking me to repeat that which I had just said. Then she typed the letter and returned it to my desk for signature. One—three—seven—twelve—eighteen errors in this one-page letter. "Keep calm," I thought, as I made corrections and returned the letter for retyping. When I got it back again, there were only six errors this time. I quietly placed it aside, and when Lisa left for the day,

I retyped the letter myself. As head of the Personnel Department, how was I going to handle this miscue?

Will All Mondays Be Like This?

Another Monday rolled around and just as the last one shaped up, this one was a repeat. In walked Dr. Vest who seated himself on the same corner of my desk, breathed deeply and with a facial muscle twitching incessantly, began to talk. "Brandon, I am sorry I got you into this mess. I haven't been able to be of any assistance, and I apologize. I'll be in the office only a few minutes today because the doctors are forcing me to go on vacation. They say that I must have some rest and relaxation. So, I'm leaving home by mid-morning and expect to be gone at least a week. We're going to the hills to try to relax. Again, I'm sorry that I've been of so little help." And without allowing time for a response, he was gone.

Facing Dogged Resistance

Three people applied for the Inservice Assistant position, so I began the interview process. All had fine credentials. Two had spent most of their careers in the Jackson schools. The third one was no newcomer, but neither was she too inbred to change. Obviously, change would be necessary, indeed great change was in the mill. Could the older, long-timers adjust, or had they become, like most of the white administrators, determined not to let desegregation work so it would go away? Then too, where would their loyalties lie? Could they support and follow an outsider, or would they listen to and heed some of the dogmatic old-timers. With a degree of reluctance, I went with the younger applicant, Hilda Lankford, a superb English teacher in the district's most outstanding high school. She was expected to begin her duties the next (shudder) Monday. Hilda was vivacious, highly energetic, bright, in her late 30's, and eager for a challenge. She had a husband and two sons. One had already graduated from high school and the other was nearing graduation. So, she would be free to travel, some of which would be a requirement for the position.

Problems were just in their infancy. Jim Minor was not only opposed to having another professional employee in the central office, but he became downright mean about it. "There's not another office space in this building so she may have to be placed in Hal Moore Annex across town.

But, I'm not worrying about it. It's your problem. You do the worrying. This whole thing is nothing but a mess, so get on out of here."

Somehow, I got the feeling that I didn't have a lot of support among the higher ups in the Jackson schools. There were a few friendly faces, but older staff members in the more powerful positions, with the exception of Al Russell, didn't wear them. Sam Arnold sometimes was more than reluctant to cooperate. He held the strings to the moneybag with exceeding closeness when I presented my needs. Then there was Johnny Wise, a black man who for years virtually ran the black schools, who was now Federal Program Director. He had a winning smile, but warned me from time to time not to appear too friendly or spend excessive time with him. "There are people here who won't appreciate it."

The Worst Monday Yet

As if every Monday was cut from the same cloth, Superintendent Vest enters again. Occupying the same desk corner for the third consecutive Monday, cup of coffee in unsteady hand, he shakes his head as an indication of great sorrow before speaking. "I can't express to you my regret of bringing you here. I've been no help or support. Other than me, you are the lone outsider here and," hesitating, "that's not good. With deepest regrets, I have to tell you I'm meeting with the staff and the press at 10:00 this morning to announce my resignation. Brandon, the doctors told me that I could walk out today or be carried out within a short time. I have no choice. I've got to resign. You'll never know how much I hate to leave you here, but I must." And he was gone.

Interim Superintendent Named

The meeting was short. Dr. Vest, visibly shaking and holding back tears, read his statement of resignation:

> *With deep regret I have found it necessary to request the Board of Trustees to accept my resignation as Superintendent of the Jackson Public Schools. As everyone is well aware, the Jackson schools have been in a continuous series of litigation involving numerous court orders requiring the Superintendent to administer drastic changes. Professionally and personally I cannot continue as Superintendent under the existing situation. I regret that*

I cannot be involved in developing the outstanding school program that I am confident could exist in Jackson. I assumed the position of Superintendent here to develop such a program. Unremitting disruption has prevented the accomplishment of that objective.

I wish to express my deep and sincere gratitude to the Board of Trustees, the teachers, administrators, and staff, the business leaders of this community, the Mayor and City Council, and to parents and students for your expressions and acts of support and confidence in me as Superintendent and in our public schools.

All citizens in this community must now work together as never before to create a public school system all can share with pride. You can accomplish this if all concerned, black and white, work cooperatively—and with reason—toward that goal. You have one of the finest and most dedicated Boards of Trustees and school staffs in the country. They will do all they possibly can to assure your children a safe and educationally rewarding school experience. Support them and each other. The prosperity, growth, and happiness of the city require it.

Bob Ross, President of the Board of Education, a huge man in his early 70's, maybe six foot four, slightly overweight, rich, powerful, gruff, prejudiced but realistic, an "in-charge" person who ran a one-man board, moved to the podium and announced that Dr. Al Russell would serve as Interim Superintendent. No mention was made of when, or if, a permanent replacement for the departing superintendent would be made. Dr. Vest's departure was so sudden that the Board, perhaps, had insufficient time to make any plans other than to name the number two person as interim superintendent.

Much surprise was displayed; however, happy faces also could be noted in the crowd. "One of our own is back in charge," could be read in selected expressions. The room was abuzz with projections and expectations, but no one there was more uncertain of what the future held for him than Brandon Sparkman.

A prominent educator described the Jackson Superintendency as the toughest job in the state of Mississippi.

Chapter 3

Wolves Attack

Tuesday morning shortly after I arrived at work, a contingent of the hungry pack entered my office. The trio included Dr. Walter Riley, Assistant Superintendent for Instruction, Lawson McCreary, Director of Secondary Schools, and Wilma Holland, Director of Elementary Schools. Wilma was new to her position, having just left an elementary principalship where she had managed a very good school. She was in her 50's, a rather large, not overweight woman, who gave the impression that she could hold her own in any battle. Dr. Riley had coaxed these two into being his backups, exhibiting strength with numbers.

Without the courtesy of a salutation, they aggressively approached their perceived prey. Walter led the attack by reminding, or more accurately assuring, me that I was new and had no knowledge of the Jackson schools and their needs. Further, he stated that the current staff (obviously excluding me) knew the schools, staff, and needs and could manage the staff development program much more effectively than I. He quickly proposed that I relinquish control of the federal grant and let him manage it, which he allowed should be a part of Instruction. The others chimed in from time to time, pointing out that those who knew the system best should direct the use of funds. Then too, they were blatant in presenting their perceived "fact" that the teachers and principals had confidence in them and had zero faith in me. "How can they trust you when they don't even know you?" Wilma questioned.

Having had my back against the wall more than once, I stared eyeball to eyeball, looking at one, then another, then the other and responding with, "No." Not believing what they had just heard, they started over, but this time more aggressively. When another "No" was heard, Walter, in particular, became angry and began to threaten, but to no avail. The calm response continued to be a simple "No."

Sensing no progress, Walter said, "Well, we'll talk with Al and have him take the grant away from you."

"Tell him he might need to talk with the Board before making that move final," I warned. The defanged wolves retreated more quickly than they had entered. And never again was the subject broached by anyone.

Power Play Foiled

With Jim Minor's secretary away from her desk, I knocked on his office door. Looking up with a scowl, Jim grumpily yelled, "Well come on in." I reminded him that I still didn't have a phone line or an office for my Inservice Assistant. "We'll do what we can do when we get around to it, and not before. Now Sam told me there was no money in the budget for a phone line, and until he tells me that the money is there, there will be **no new phone line**." I turned and walked down the hall to Sam Arnold's office where I inquired about progress on securing the line. Sam responded as he had previously, that there was no money in the budget for additional phone lines, and that none would be made available without a written request to the Board, which would have to be approved by Superintendent Russell.

With anger showing, I glared into the eyes of Sam. "There are 1.3 million dollars in my budget, and I **will** have a phone line within one week. If you have questions or problems see me. I can make it move if I have to." Unhurriedly, I arose from my seat and walked out. Two days later I had a private telephone line.

Hilda Lankford, having no desk or office, occupied the only extra chair in my office while working from the end of my desk. Her purse and working materials were stacked on the floor. I was not embarrassed by perhaps being the only assistant superintendent in America required to share a tiny office and desk with an assistant. But the problem was the inefficiency and hassle of the arrangement. Several times each day when I needed privacy for talking with someone, conducting an interview, or discussing sensitive matters by phone, Hilda left the office and occupied a vacant chair in the Personnel Office waiting area. Obviously, Hilda couldn't do her job effectively and neither could I under these conditions.

When the central office had cleared for the day, I surveyed the different offices and storage areas until he found a desk not being used. I literally dragged the desk to a place in the hallway just outside my office. There I deposited the desk and placed beside it an old, beat-up file cabinet I had found in the adjoining warehouse. I took the extra chair from my office and scooted it under the desk. That evening, from my motel room, I called Hilda, explained what I had done, and told her that would be her temporary office.

The next morning, Jim Minor entered the central office and swaggered along the hallway, rounded the corner, then stopped cold. There sat Hilda working at the desk I had provided. Sam turned abruptly, stamped into my office and blurted, "What's that desk doing in that hall?"

"That's Hilda's office," I explained.

Jim, shouting loudly and with fist slamming the desk, "That hallway belongs to me, and there will be no desk in it. Do you understand?"

I arose from my chair slowly, walked around the desk and with my face about six inches from Sam's face I exploded. "I have put up with this pack of wolves as long as I intend to. I've whipped a few butts in my time, and I've had mine whipped a time or two. And right now I'm going to see what you have behind that grouchy, smart mouth." My 5' 11", 170 pounds next to Jim's 6' 4", 265 would appear to be a "no contest", but I knew that a person who rules by intimidation doesn't have a backbone. But I didn't recall that little bit of knowledge prior to acting. I was fed up and angry and to heck with the outcome.

With that, Jim's countenance fell, and he began backing away quickly saying, "No, no. I'm sorry. We'll get an office for her and fix yours up today. Fire regulations won't let us have a desk in the hall, but we'll do something now."

Well, do you know what? Jim invited me into his office; got me a cup of coffee, apologized again, and asked me to prepare a list of everything I needed in the way of furniture and equipment for my office and Hilda's. He said, "I'll work with Sam and we'll get you whatever you need. Sam will know what we can get with grant money and what we'll need from local funds." As if he needed to calm the waters even more, he asked me if he could have an hour or two of my time. With a positive response, Jim said, "Be in my office in 30 minutes with the list and I'll show you around.

He took me on a tour of Jackson, driving by every school and every piece of property owned by the Jackson School District while explaining details of each property and offering comments about each school. When I returned to my office after lunch, an office furniture dealer was waiting for me. He had three executive chairs for me to examine, and possibly select one, along with a catalogue for use in selecting other items needed. He assured both Hilda and me that whatever we selected would be delivered that afternoon. And it was.

The next morning Hilda moved into her office space in the Personnel Department. Not only did she have an office with furniture, but an office adjourning hers was allocated for her secretary, whenever one was employed. The clouds lifted in the central office, and I could see a little sunshine for a change—inside that is—but outside the moisture continued to fall.

Another Desegregation Plan Assignment

Al Russell's secretary called my office and asked me to report to the Superintendent ASAP. Dr. Russell said, "Sparkman, I know you have a full plate but I'm asking you to work with the administrative staff here in drawing up an elementary desegregation plan. They're floundering and you may be able to give them some suggestions. They're meeting right now in the boardroom, so join them as soon as you can." Returning to my office to get a writing pad, I wondered if the Acting Superintendent realized that this was my third committee assignment for helping design a desegregation plan.

As I entered the boardroom and seated myself in one of the vacant chairs, my presence was largely ignored. Within half an hour, I knew I was wasting my time. The ideas being incorporated on paper were naïve: things at which the plaintiff would scoff. When I would offer an idea, it was rejected without comment or discussion, except for derision on one occasion. These people were certain that some way or other they could derail the desegregation process. It was the same old song that had been played all over the south for years. "If we don't let it work, it'll go away." Having lost eleven court battles out of eleven, they still hadn't learned that sometimes compromise is preferable to total defeat.

I knew that my presence was required at each of the committee meetings. I also determined that my primary role with the administration group and the Biracial Committee would be to show up and shut up. There was no hope for progress with either, and the less I agitated, the better off I would be. But, the other committee, or group, was different. They were sincere in trying to find a compromise position acceptable to the Plaintiff, Board and court. The Judge was tired of having his decisions overturned by the Fifth Circuit Court of Appeals, and was as serious as cancer about the Board and Plaintiff reaching an agreement so peace could prevail.

The business and professional members of this group, who obviously had the backing of the white power structure, were prominent people, including bankers, successful business owners, CEO's of large corporations, researchers, and others. These, along with the consulting group that had been diverted temporarily from their primary task to attend to this problem, understood the atmosphere and fully intended to find a solution. The consultants interviewed people all over the city—black, white, rich and poor. They were determined to arrive at a plan that would fly.

I was more of an observer than a participant although I expressed my opinions and concerns from time to time. My greatest concern was that much that was going into the plan was unsound from an educational standpoint. Many of the components would continue to drive white students into private and parochial schools. This experience was not shockingly new for me. I had seen plans before, that instead of bringing the races together, had created a greater divide that would take several generations, if ever, to overcome.

I spent many hours in meetings while what-to-do-in-order-to-gain-court-approval was bantered back and forth. Little progress was made except in the group of business people and consultants. While I attended every meeting of this later group, I was never sure that Interim Superintendent Russell was aware of my participation or even that the group existed. At no time did anyone in the central office ever mention the group. With the exit of Dr. Vest, I wondered if anyone in a position of authority knew what was going on other than the Board's attorney. As the group worked, no one ever mentioned reporting to or getting feedback from any source in the administrative office. In these sessions, I witnessed some of the sharpest minds I had ever encountered. The consultants certainly didn't have a monopoly on brains.

Other Dilemmas

Back in the office, Sandra, sympathetic with my secretarial dilemma, offered a solution. "I can place your secretary in another position where she can be more successful and let you hire another one," she suggested. "I have what looks like a good applicant. Helen Morrow has substantial experience, is about 45, neat, and highly recommended by former employers. If you would like to interview her, I'll make an appointment for tomorrow." With an affirmative nod, I was on the road to a better life in my office.

But peace was not a permanent fixture for me. The summer workshops were over, and a meeting of key central office instructional personnel was called so that Ron Seely, head consultant for staff development, could present his plans for the coming school year. Ron was in his late 40's, average height, glasses that were almost constantly in motion traveling from eyes to top of head and returning. He was a university professor whose greatest success had been in classrooms where theory was more highly applauded than performance. He was also well published. Ron stood before a portable stand that held a large multi-page pad on which he would draw a diagram, flip the page over and draw another one. He philosophized, and theorized endlessly while drawing other charts and diagrams. For sure, Ron knew all the latest educational jargon. I understood that which was happening for I had just completed the doctoral program where professors used the same terms and techniques, but few of them had been inside a public school classroom during the past 20 years. Most were clueless about how to convert their verbiage into effective practice.

After being totally confused with the one-way presentation and disillusioned with the lack of practicality, I said, "I don't understand what you are talking about."

Ron retorted, "What part don't you understand?"

"None of it," I abruptly replied.

"Well, let's go over it again," Ron said. And so he proceeded. After another half hour, Ron asked, "Do you understand now?"

"No," was repeated again.

"Well, if you don't understand that explanation, I don't believe you are capable of handling your responsibilities here," Ron said in a tone reflecting his vast superiority.

With that statement, the meeting ended, and when the others had departed, Ron and I had a parting conversation. The last thing teachers and principals in Jackson needed were diagrams, philosophies and theories. With teary eyes, teachers were begging for help in the classrooms where they no longer knew how to meet the basic educational needs of youngsters.

A Real Home at Last

The home we had purchased in North Jackson was finally vacated, and our family moved in. Having little knowledge of the area, we were excited about our new home. Located in an upscale neighborhood, all of the homes were rather large and attractive with yards that were beautifully landscaped and maintained almost to perfection. Trees were scattered throughout the locality. Our house was well designed and constructed by master craftsmen who added little conveniences uncommon to most homes. The four bedrooms fit the family size, and a formal dining room made the house almost perfect for us since we entertained frequently. Our new home was located in an area where no one had to scramble for rent money and few, if any, worried about the source for house payments. The neighborhood residents were upper middle class who didn't like the wave that was about to engulf them, and most chose to "protect" their children from the perceived damnation of the schools. So, there was no "house warming" for the new neighbors.

It seemed like a year since the family had spent more than two days together. So this was a much-celebrated event, especially for me.

The sky never remains clear forever, so difficult questions began to arise in the minds of the Sparkman family. Where would the children attend school? The temporary desegregation plan placed Ricky at a large, nearby high school which served a growing area of Jackson. The school was well run, and parents were happy with the education their children received. The exception was those who could not accept their children attending a desegregated school.

Not far away was the elementary school where Robert would enter first grade. This, again, was a well-run school of about 400 pupils. As in all schools, the student body and staff had been fully integrated the last semester of the preceding school year. Every black teacher was teamed with a white teacher of the same grade, thus requiring "team teaching".

The previous year, Robert had attended a private kindergarten that didn't teach reading skills to children, but otherwise he was well prepared and anxious to get in regular school. He was expected to do well in first grade.

But Rita would have to go across town and attend a single grade school certain to be populated mostly by black students. This was previously an all-black high school where discipline had been a problem and academic achievement was less than acceptable. This school was changed by the court to serve tenth grade only, an arrangement that no one liked except the judges.

How would Rita fit in? Would she be happy? Would she learn effectively? Would her emotional stability be endangered? After lengthy discussions, Wanda and I determined that Rita would attend the assigned school. If the academic level of instruction was unacceptable, she would be tutored. If her emotional well-being were endangered, she would be withdrawn and placed in a private school. I realized that such a move would endanger my job, but the emotional welfare of my family was more important than any position. As one knowing Rita might surmise, she had no dread or fear of attending this school.

Sunday was church day for our family, so off we went to a nearby, rather large Methodist church. We arrived in time for Sunday school, and with some friendly help, each member found a class. When Wanda and I were introduced, it was if cold water had been poured on the group. As the lesson trailed to a discussion, racial remarks began to ooze out. Before the class ended, angry statements and feelings of frustration would have received much higher marks than the intended lesson outcome.

We attended the 11 a.m. service, but conversations between Sunday school and the service, as well as after the service, told us we were not welcome there. North Jackson was an affluent community with people who could afford private school tuition, and they were completely turned off by the public schools and anyone who supported them. The next Sunday we would try another church, then perhaps another and another until we could find one where our worship each week would not be stained by racism and hatred.

Eventually the family decided to try Galloway Methodist church, the conference headquarters church near downtown and the capitol. This was a large church with a big staff, accustomed to welcoming newcomers who could be absorbed into the congregation without undue attention.

Galloway had a healthy mixture of conservatives and liberals, old line families, transients and new members. At last, our family had found a church home. With the family together and a welcoming church, for me, the sun began to shine through the clouds. Suddenly, I began to see the city of Jackson as it really was: Highly attractive.

Although large in area and population, it had the feel of a small town. Autumn was in the air, and the abundance of trees added greatly to its beauty. The residential part of the city was somewhat divided into communities separated by wooded areas, and most of the areas were dotted with trees which added beauty and a peaceful nature to the neighborhoods. Then some distance away would be another close-knit community.

Major roads and interstate highways dissecting the city afforded even greater separation of residential areas. The presence of autumn colors throughout Jackson made it one of the most attractive cities that could be found. Because of the absence of family, seemingly unending rain, and the awareness of mounting school problems, I had totally missed the positives that Jackson had to offer.

Housing in Jackson was still almost totally segregated. Northeast Jackson was home of the white elite. There were some middle class neighborhoods, but it was populated largely by the more wealthy, educated and influential. South Jackson was more of a white, middle class community with separate neighborhoods designed much the same as North Jackson. There too was an abundance of trees. West Jackson, including Northwest Jackson, was populated largely by black people. While most of this region contained trees, they were fewer in number, and it didn't have the separation of neighborhoods to the same extent as did the other residential areas of the city. There was an absence of affluence here that was found elsewhere, and the black region was interspersed with ghetto areas. Most of these areas had their own school or schools. There was no East Jackson because that side of town was nestled near Pearl River.

Downtown Jackson was clean and attractive with a moderate but impressive skyline. Capitol Street was the main drag through the business district, terminating at the old state capitol. Prominent along this street was the old Heidelberg Hotel which housed most of the large gatherings requiring meals. Several large banks were interspersed among retail stores. St. Andrews church was an attractive addition to the downtown area as was the Governor's Mansion. Central High School, Galloway Methodist Church, First Baptist Church, state office buildings and the state capitol dominated a large section adjoining the downtown business district. A nice, large coliseum which allowed significant entertainment was approximately four blocks east of the old capitol. Then just south of Capitol Street was a large auditorium where the community had access to presentations by the Jackson Symphony Orchestra and other fine arts events.

Jackson had acquired a very negative reputation largely because of its struggle with integration. However, once familiar with, and accustomed to the city, I found Jackson to be one of the most progressive cities in America, with unusually solid and progressive leaders.

Chapter 4

Renewed Focus

It was like the beginning of a new school year every two or three months in the Jackson schools. The constant changes in school assignments for students and teachers brought on by new court orders required almost starting from scratch. And so it was in September 1970. The reshuffling between terms saw new faces everywhere. Several of the schools, prior to January 1970, were considered outstanding by any measure. Quality was the result of principals organizing well, hiring outstanding teachers and supervising and supporting their work. Now most principals had no more than 60% of the teachers that had been recommended and hired for that school.

The level of achievement within each school ranged from non-readers to those whose academic achievement ranked in the 99th percentile nationally. How could the old system of teaching everyone the same thing at the same time serve this broad range of achievers? Most teachers were totally frustrated and some were begging for help. A large percentage of parents and others in the city were convinced that the schools were in total disarray, and thought by many to be dangerous. Teaching and learning had been neglected by the central office staff because of what appeared to be problems more pressing than instruction. Never since arriving in Jackson had I heard the word "Instruction" mentioned in central office staff meetings. This was a situation ripe for change.

Plan for Change

I called two friends who had worked with me as consultants in Tuscumbia, Alabama. Dr. Joe Richardson, a professor at Georgia State University, had grown up professionally in some of the finest schools in America and had received his doctorate from Northwestern University. A friend through happenstances, he and his family had spent several spring vacations in a waterfront home I had arranged for them to use. Dr. Richardson had recommended outstanding consultants during my tenure as Assistant Superintendent in Tuscumbia, when I was dealing with desegregation related problems. He also had conducted workshops and coordinated large summer teacher training events for the district.

The other person called was Dr. Jon Kinghorn, a genius at finding the "bottom line" in a flash. He offered no flowery speeches, but would lay the situation out in simple, easy to understand form. The simplicity of his proposed solutions astounded those around him. Jon was a doctoral student at Indiana University when I first met him. A professor At IU, who had agreed to work as a consultant in the district, had a conflict so he sent Jon as his replacement. His work was so impressive that I used him as a consultant several times before he graduated and even after he went to work with the Charles F. Kettering Foundation in Dayton, Ohio. Jon was small in stature physically, unimpressive in appearance, but a mental giant.

Joe, Jon and Hilda met with me two consecutive days as we hammered out a plan of attack. The teaching staff must understand how to deal with more than one level of achievers in the same classroom without shortchanging anyone. Having been accustomed to teaching the same thing to everyone at the same time, this new concept was going to be difficult for the staff to grasp and implement. Fortunately, a grouping and regrouping approach to teaching (some called it Individualized Instruction) was being used successfully in many places in America. So it was not a new, radical idea and was greatly needed in Jackson. The consensus plan involved several steps and processes.

1. The new concept must be presented by consultants to all principals and teachers in a clear, succinct manner and pursued until thoroughly grasped.

Jackson Public Schools. Many residents of the city openly questioned if there would be a public school system in Jackson after the end of the current school year. This work was critical, and every person in the group of about 15 realized the gravity of each decision made. I assumed that many of the local business people in the group felt much as I did about parts of the plan but had the courage to ignore acquired understanding, and perhaps even lay aside prejudices. The task that had been assigned to me was difficult, but I repeatedly reminded myself that I didn't come to Jackson for a picnic.

At Home

On the home front, all was not bad. We had one friendly neighbor on each side. Beyond that, we were pretty much kept at arm's length. The Lt. Governor, William Winter, whose daughter was in the same class as Rita, befriended her by, among other things, inviting her to attend the first football game of the season with the Winter family.

At the end of the second day of football practice, Ricky came home and said, "Daddy, I'm going to quit football. I've missed three weeks of practice, and I'm so far behind that I'll never catch up. Besides that, they have good players, and I'm not sure I can help the team."

"You never really liked the sport, so I think this is a good time to call it quits," I replied.

Because of the shortage of substitute teachers, Wanda offered to perform that service and was called for duty rather regularly. Ricky had a good senior year in high school, and even played the role of a major character in a local theater production. He put his painting experience to work painting houses with the help of a cute girlfriend who did the detailed work while he covered the flat surfaces. Rita was happy in her school even though she had as few as one other white student in some classes and only three in some others. Academically, her program was somewhat anemic, but the family felt that she could survive this one year without noticeable detriment to her educational goals.

Robert's experience was another matter. He had a team of two teachers, one white and the other black. The white teacher, who dominated the team, appeared to have severe emotional problems and was so strict and demanding that students found school to be a very debilitating experience. Her students were not allowed to talk, even in the hallways or lunchroom.

The only time they had permission to say anything to each other was on the playground. Had it not been for the gentle, loving nature of the large, black, teacher, whose speech and writings were regularly punctuated with grammatical errors, Robert would have had to be withdrawn. He was developing serious insecurity behaviors that were worrisome to Wanda and me. While not in school, he neared the point of hysteria any time a member of the family was not in his sight, even if momentarily. The black teacher was extremely weak in teaching skills, but her love and concern for the children made her inadequacies easy to overlook.

Graduation time for Ricky was only a few months away, and Wanda and I became concerned about college expenses. Even though I was making more money than ever, even with frugal living, it still took every dime I earned for us to live. Ricky wanted to attend school at the University of Alabama. The thought of him being an out of state student caused a great quandary about the financial future of the family.

Trips for Special Training

Delay in obtaining materials and equipment tried the patience of teachers and principals. After an order would be placed for teaching material, it was not uncommon for months to pass before delivery. Money in the federal grant I was administering had to be spent by the end of the fiscal year, yet purchases would be requested early in the school year and the materials not arrive for several months.

I invited Sam Arnold and Mike Israel, Director of Computer Services to accompany me on a trip to Chattanooga, a school district of similar size that had a well-designed computer managed purchasing, warehouse control and delivery system. Mike, a 30 year old, tall, somewhat handsome, egotistical, self-aggrandizing, former math teacher, had been assigned to initiate a computer system capable of handling several critical functions of the district, especially, accounting and inventory.

We arrived in the city the evening before the scheduled visit and spent the night in a motel suite not far from the district office. The next morning while I was combing my hair, Mike walked up behind me, tousled my hair and sarcastically said to Sam, "If I had hair like his, I'd get a toupee." Silently, I re-combed my hair.

The visit was an eye opener for everyone. Certainly this system could revolutionize the purchasing and delivery system for Jackson. While

Sam showed an interest and asked good questions, Mike was detached, regularly making snide remarks to Sam. After returning to Jackson, if any knowledge gained was applied to the Jackson situation, I never heard about it. Certainly, no effort was made to utilize the seldom-used computer to improve this ill-functioning area.

Human Relations Skills Training

There was daily conflict in some junior and senior high schools that seldom turned into fights, but created tension and insecurity in the student body and faculty. Lack of human relations skills was a definite factor undermining stability and achievement in many of the Jackson schools.

I determined that these problems would die slowly unless attitudinal changes could be accelerated in these troubled schools. Accordingly, I arranged with the Charles F. Kettering foundation to provide training for key administrators and consultants who would then work with teachers, and students, offering ways of resolving differences. I accompanied the group to Ohio for training in "conflict resolution" and in "human relations skills." This training proved to be valuable once the participants held work sessions with large numbers of teachers, and in turn, used the newly acquired skills with their students.

A Line is Drawn

With the staff development program proceeding smoothly, I decided to have an orientation session with central office administrators to help them understand the direction of the program so all, or most, could be on the same page. Lead consultants representing each area of staff development work spoke to the group, explaining key concepts of the changes being made. At the end of all presentations, an opportunity was given for comments and questions.

Sam Arnold seized the moment and proceeded to inform the group that the whole staff development program and direction represented a major step backward and was a total farce. He raved on for about five minutes then quickly left the room. I stepped to the podium and offered reassurance of the need, validity and effectiveness of the program. A great disciple of Dr. Prince, Sam had attempted to say that anything, other than that which had been done in the past, was heretical. This incident tended to meld the defenders of the status quo.

Grant Extension Critical

As work continued on the desegregation plan, one fact became clear. Much additional money would be needed. Then too, while a lot of progress had been made in staff training, it would take several years to implement and institutionalize a quality instructional program. Old habits die slowly, and they are especially lingering and painful at the high school level, so a new grant proposal had to be prepared.

I outlined the proposal, listing needs and justification. Hilda took the lead in writing the narrative portion. After the requests were prepared in rough form, Seth Rutherford, a business member of the desegregation planning team, told me to set my sights high because he had assurance from the White House that the cost of bussing and related expenses would be borne by the federal government. Seth was CEO of a huge industry. Not only had his company made large contributions to President Nixon's campaign fund, he also had close friends in the President's Cabinet.

Back at the drawing board, a new design of the proposal was in the making. The state Research and Development Center staff, adept at proposal writing, offered valuable assistance. The cost of 70 new busses, salaries of drivers, fuel for operating the busses, and maintenance were added to the budget. Additionally, money was added for construction of the North Plaza. The new total requested reached the $ 2,000,000 mark. If approved, the grant would consume most of the funds reserved by Congress for the state of Mississippi.

Desegregation Plan Takes Shape

Work of the consulting firm in surveying the community began to pay dividends. Clearly, parents of both races wanted stability in the schools. Additionally, they wanted to return to the 1-6, 7-9 and 10-12 grade structures they were accustomed to having. They detested the court-ordered single grade schools. The black community didn't want to bear the brunt of bussing. The white community was unwilling for their children to attend schools in neighborhoods they considered unsafe, or at least had the appearance of so being. Neither were they willing for their children to attend some of the old, poorly maintained, buildings, formerly housing black students. With this information, the group went to work incorporating these concepts, to the extent possible.

School Board Attorney, Artie Ulmus, was invited to attend a work session to evaluate the projected direction of the planners, as well as the tentative details already on paper. Additionally, he was asked to offer suggestions for elements to include in the plan that would be required for meeting plaintiff's demands.

It now became obvious that Artie Ulmus was the key player for the Board in deciding which plan to offer the court, and in negotiating with the NAACP Legal Defense Fund and the Biracial Committee, each of which must approve the plan. More schools than originally planned would need to be closed. The group arrived at a decision to recommend closure of nine schools. Some of these were in good condition and would have served well for many years, but the list of closures could not be limited to formerly black schools.

Attempting to adhere to traditional 1-6 grade schools as nearly as possible, it was discovered that eight schools could serve that grade span and, through zoning, be projected to attain the "magic" black/white ratio required by court decree. Staying as close to tradition as possible, 20 schools serving grades 1-4 could be expected to meet requirements through careful zoning. With the closing of nine schools, space became a prime consideration. Where could all of the students be housed? Also, the selling factor had to be considered. What approach must be taken to sell the plan to the community, and especially the white population? Using numbers supplied by the school district statistician, and ignoring financial constraints, the planners came up with the idea of building two large education centers to house 5th and 6th grade students who otherwise would attend the 20 grade 1-4 schools. These could be called Plazas, with large open spaces, utilizing team teaching and other progressive and creative approaches to dispensing knowledge. One of the plazas would be located in North Jackson and the other in South Jackson. They were to be built as soon as possible.

Transportation necessary for carrying out the plan was a must; therefore, bussing, a forbidden term in Mississippi (except for White Citizen Council Schools, to which white busses ran) was made a formal part of the plan. Accordingly, students living more than 1 ½ miles from school were entitled to transportation. Not only would this provision be extremely controversial, but also where would the half million dollars to pay for this service come from? Any concern about financing the proposed ideas was brushed aside as if totally insignificant. After all, the deadline was approaching for presenting the plan, and quality education for students was not allowed to interfere with, what at the time, was perceived to be a much greater need.

The stability factor had not yet been dealt with. What could be included in the plan that would stop all of the court interference and constant reconfiguration of Jackson's schools?

"Let's put in a provision that no further litigation can be filed for a period of five years," one member proposed. Artie Ulmus was called back in to look at the plan.

"They'll never buy the five year clause," Ulmus stated emphatically. After further discussion, the five years was reduced to three and became a part of the plan.

Negotiation Begins

Now the major undertaking was to parlay an agreement between the Board of Education and the Biracial Committee that was dominated by Justin Cohen. The big plan drawn up by the business and consulting group was just the beginning of things to be negotiated. Plaintiffs wanted some changes in this plan, but were more interested in details for implementing the plan. What was to be done with the closed schools? What would be the racial makeup of the administrators and supervisors at the Education plazas? What would be the wording of the press release announcing an agreement on the plan? How will peace and security on busses be assured? If the plaintiffs agree to not challenge the plan for three years, what will be the role of the District Court in the matter? What will happen if the plan fails to achieve a unitary school system? These were questions requiring clarification in writing, with Board and Biracial Committee approval. This was the hard part.

Artie Ulmus and Justin Cohen poured over these points incessantly. With each new draft, neither the Board of Education nor Cohen could agree, as reported by Ulmus. The court deadline was at hand and no agreement had been reached. I became antsy. I was certain that there would be a deadlock and the court would impose the HEW plan: a deathblow to the Jackson Public Schools. I was disenchanted with the Jackson School System and was rueful of the day I asked for a job there.

Unauthorized Attempt to Save Plan

Having tossed and turned in bed most of Friday night, I arose and ate breakfast with the family. Turning to Wanda, I said, "I'm going to see Cohen this morning."

Totally shocked she responded, "Why in the world would you do that?"

"The plan is not going to be accepted by either side unless someone intervenes," was my reply.

"Well, who are you to intervene, and who authorized you to intervene?" she asked curtly.

"No one has even mentioned it to me, but the plan will not be accepted unless someone makes the effort to save it," I stated.

"According to you, the plan is terrible. Why would you do such a foolish thing in order to save something so impractical?" she insisted. "Doing this could get you fired," Wanda begged.

"OK, maybe it will, but unless something is done this weekend, the Jackson Schools will go down the drain, and as far as my being fired is concerned, let'em do it, and I'll be the winner," I told her as I arose from the table.

Picking up my jacket and sliding an arm in a sleeve, I walked out the door. As I drove toward downtown Jackson I felt huge balls churning inside my stomach. In the seat beside me was a paper I had secured that had the eight sticking points of the plan. I didn't mind talking with Cohen nearly as much as I dreaded getting into his office. I had never been in that part of town before, except when driving through in my car. And another problem was determining which building housed the lawyer.

Cohen's office was in a dilapidated part of the city where blacks regularly hung out in droves, and one could hear the boisterous language and laughter all the way to Capitol Street, the main downtown thoroughfare. Having little experience in this type of setting, I was uneasy about my physical safety. Things were tense between blacks and whites in Jackson; therefore, I wondered where I could park my car, and how I could navigate through the crowd safely. Then it occurred to me that I would have no trouble if I were to park near Cohen's office and be seen entering. And that's just what I did.

Climbing the dirty, stained, unusually long, dangerously worn, antique stairway, I wondered if I was in the right place. The number on the building indicated that it was, but it sure didn't resemble any lawyer's office I had ever seen. I kept climbing and upon reaching the top, I slowly turned the doorknob, pushed the door open and entered. There was little noticeable difference in the qualities of the office and the stairs I had just climbed—dirty looking, unclean walls and ceiling, and sparse furnishings.

A young black woman seated behind a desk asked if she could help me. Convinced that my facial expressions and color revealed my apprehension, I said, "I'm Brandon Sparkman, and I'd like to see Mr. Cohen." Without responding she left her desk and went into an adjoining room where the door had been closed.

After what seemed like ten minutes, she emerged saying, "He's busy. If you want to see him you will have to wait."

"That's fine," I offered, and then walked to the back of the unusually long office where I seated myself on a well-worn sofa, the only seat available in this rag tag office which had no pictures or paintings on the walls, and there were no other decorations. The worn, pine floor appeared to have been neglected for years. Additionally, there were no reading materials anywhere. Time was going to pass slowly with nothing to do except sit and wait, or reread the two-page document I had brought with me. Time would pass, but that time would be long and painful.

Obviously, there were three people in the office complex: me, Cohen and his secretary. Cohen and I had had a major confrontation early on. There had been little or no conversation between us since that incident, because I had fulfilled my plan of "show up and shut up" at the Biracial Committee meetings. I had talked only when questioned by a member of the Committee, and I did that as concisely and non-committal as possible. Cohen didn't really know me and my tenacity. If this lawyer thought I would get discouraged and leave, then he was plain wrong. Even though it was mid-morning, I was prepared to help him lockup if that's what it took.

Final Negotiations

The clock kept ticking and I kept squirming. "What if that so-and-so calls me in and proceeds to berate me, talk in legalese and be as defiant as he was at our first meeting?" I thought. "I'll not let his behavior get to me. I'll be polite but persistent in presenting concession possibilities and in arguing their merits". I was determined to push the concept that the education and welfare of children were paramount. An hour passed and not one word was heard. Or maybe it had been more than an hour, or was it just a half-hour that seemed like an hour. The secretary appeared to be equally uneasy. She would type a few words, shuffle some papers, turn her back to me, but never cast a glance in my direction.

Hearing a door open and footsteps, I rose to my feet and turned to greet the most hated man in Mississippi. Rather than inviting me into his office, he seated himself on the sagging sofa and asked, "Now what can I do for you?" I explained that I understood the two sides had failed to agree on certain matters and that I was greatly concerned for the education and welfare of the students, both black and white. I handed Cohen a copy of the eight unresolved issues and initiated a discussion of the first item. After an explanation of his concern, and my response, Cohen asked that a clarifying statement be inserted and then he accepted that item.

On the second item, the attorney said that he and Ulmus had discussed the issue and had modified the wording so that it was okay with him. He accepted that item also. When an impasse was reached, rather than pushing the issue, I would suggest that the item be set aside for later discussion. This process of looking at each item and discussing the pros and cons as well as the wording resulted in rewording some items for clarification and a degree of modification of intent of one such item. After going over the eighth item, I directed our attention to the ones that had been skipped because of preliminary disagreement. After perhaps an hour or so, all items had been covered thoroughly and Cohen had agreed on five of them. Then he began writing other demands on his yellow legal pad, such as the Board of Education must maintain the abandoned schools and the city must find meaningful uses for them that will serve the needs of the communities; that monitors be provided on busses to assure order and discipline; that a proportionate number of blacks be assigned to administrative positions in the plazas; and that the Board prepare a press release with affirmative language supportive of constructing the plazas.

"That's it," he said. "I have conceded five of the eight and if there is any agreement, the Board will relent on the other three." We shook hands and I glided gingerly down the stairs with another stop on my mind

As I emerged into the noise on the sidewalk, bodies began to part, forming a pathway for my retreat to my parked car. (I was relieved to see that there was no damage). I eased down the street until devoid of glaring eyes, turned right, circled a couple of blocks and crossed Capitol Street into a different world.

Agreement Reached

Entering the outer office of Fred Ware, a name familiar to all in Mississippi, several people in this newspaper office, with desks jammed closely, were typing frantically on this warm, sunny Saturday morning. Materials were stacked around cumbersomely with typewriters singing, which indicated they were trying to meet a deadline. The lady seated nearest the door, small in stature, wearing a black and red plaid dress, horn rimmed glasses, and a "don't interrupt me" countenance, stopped typing momentarily. "May I help you?" she inquired.

"I'm Brandon Sparkman. I'd like to see Mr. Ware," I replied.

The lady picked up the phone receiver, pressed a button and said, "Mr. Ware, a Mr. Brandon Sparkman is here and would like to speak with you." Almost immediately a door at the end of a short hall to my left opened and Fred Ware, a man of average height, trim and perhaps in his 60's, motioned for me to enter. Fred Ware was a member of a prominent, wealthy, dynasty with almost unlimited influence in Jackson and in the state.

The office was adequately appointed but cluttered with unfinished paperwork. Fred Ware greeted me warmly, and then seated himself behind his desk as I selected one of the two chairs on the opposite side. I could observe that Ware was caught by surprise by the inquiring look on his face.

"I know you are wondering why I am here, and I'm about as unsure as you are," I began. "I have no authority to be here. No one suggested I do what I'm doing today, but we have a crisis on our hands and somebody has to do something about it, so here I am. The Board and Justin Cohen have not agreed on eight provisions of the desegregation plan, so I have taken it on myself to try to get a compromise. If this plan isn't jointly presented to the court next Tuesday, the HEW plan will be imposed, and that will completely destroy our schools. I have just come from Justin's office where he conceded five of the eight controversial points and said he would not accept the other three. He said the Board would have to yield on those or there would be no agreement. I am told that the Board is divided and unwilling to yield on any of the plaintiff's modifications. Unless someone intervenes, we are going down the drain," I explained.

In a grumpy and demanding voice, Ware responded, "Give me that paper. What is it Cohen won't accept?"

Pointing out the items which Cohen had agreed to and the three which he had rejected, I said, "These are the ones we have to work on, Mr. Ware."

Fred Ware jumped to his feet, and shouted angrily, "I don't like this. I don't like any part of this. This whole damned thing is ridiculous and destructive. I hate it." With Fred having vented his anger, I picked the document up and was ready to leave when Ware said, "The two board members who are holding this thing up are Bob and Helen. They have refused to budge. Let me make a copy of that thing. I'll see that it's done." Handing me the original after making a copy, he said, "Thank you."

And with that done, I left the office of one who made things happen and kept things from happening. Fred Ware was rich, powerful, and influential beyond belief.

Mayor Responds

Monday morning Mayor Richard Miles, a tall, trim, handsome, progressive, easy to know man in his late 40's, penned a letter to Justin Cohen and had it hand delivered immediately.

Dear (Mr. Cohen):

It is our privilege to advise you that the City of Jackson is prepared at once to make plans for the use of Jones Elementary School and Martin Elementary School as community centers. These plans will be completed and implemented with dispatch and with the unqualified support of my office. Our present ideas regarding the type of activities which might be conducted at the site would encompass the following:

> *Day care*
> *Study and Reading*
> *Indoor Play Program*
> *Emergency food*
> *Nutrition Programs*
> *Family Planning*
> *Adult Education*
> *Public Welfare Programs*
> *Alcohol Counter Measures*
> *Medical Clinic*
> *Youth Court Counseling and Corrections*
> *Civil Defense Classes*

I would personally welcome any ideas which you or residents of the neighborhoods might have regarding the above activities or other programs which might be desirable. On behalf of the City Council I would like to acknowledge that we have received from the Trustees of the Jackson Municipal Separate School District a firm recommendation that other closed facilities retained by the School District should be used for community service centers, providing a variety of services. You may be assured that we will give this recommendation our most careful consideration.

Yours very truly

Final Court Order Delivered

I never knew to whom the document approved by Cohen, and the yellow sheets signed by him, were given. I heard nothing else official, but in the local newspaper the following Monday, an article appeared quoting an unnamed source as saying the desegregation plan had been approved by both the Board and the Biracial Committee and would be presented to the District Court for acceptance. The next day an article also identified many of the provisions of the plan including the transportation requirement. Then on Tuesday, the court approved the plan and ordered immediate implementation. In early July, busses for transporting 9,000 students for implementing the plan were ordered and driver vacancy positions were posted.

Consulting Firm Explains Basis for Plan

The Manager of the T.E.M.P.O. team said his people spent hundreds of hours talking with principals, teachers, parents, students, organizations, and leaders of both black and white communities. The general conclusion reached by the team was that the schools in Jackson were in a crisis situation that required extreme actions to preserve a good school system. The team concluded that, (1) the educational aspects of school planning had been lost or overlooked in desegregation plans addressing the degree of integration rather than sound educational programs; (2) the black community was committed to substantial integration of all schools; (3) there was a strong sentiment for restoring stability and discarding the ever changing attendance zones and grade structures; (4) whites in many instances would accept integrated schools for their children but in some circumstances would not. While there were varying degrees of resistance and for various reasons, a session and a half under massive integration indicated that whites would not attend schools in certain neighborhoods and schools in which the age and condition of the building were considered undesirable; (5) black parents were concerned about a school plan which imposes upon their children a transportation problem; (6) the black community also was concerned about the possibility of closing only formerly black schools; and (7) both blacks and whites deplored the abandonment of the 6-3-3 grade structure.

There was much criticism of the secondary school plan. It's conceded that both plaintiffs and defendants would take a close look at the secondary school plan before another session begins. However, because of the extensive conferences on the elementary school plan, talks on it have not yet begun. Presumably, some agreement will be sought on this plan before it goes back before the court.

Relief Envisioned

Meanwhile on the home front the Sparkman family faced another daunting problem. In a parent conference, Wanda was notified by one of Robert's teachers that he would be unable to go to second grade the following school year unless he attended summer school for remedial work. That evening when Wanda informed me of the bombshell, I was livid. "That poor kid has had nothing but hell all year. His unbelievable experiences have almost destroyed him emotionally, and I'm not sending him to summer school. What he needs is fun and relaxation and that's that," I exploded.

"What'll we do?" Wanda questioned.

"Nothing," was my response.

"Will you go talk with the teachers?" she wanted to know.

"No, we'll just wait and see what happens," I said with finality.

With that problem settled, at least temporarily, that evening the family began planning a vacation. By consensus, we would make a two week camping trip with visits to Williamsburg, Charlottesville and Washington, D.C., culminating with a few days in New York City. Rita was elated about the New York part because she had always wanted to see some Broadway plays. Our family had developed a close friendship with a consultant from Northeastern Pennsylvania, who upon learning of the vacation plan, suggested we not attempt to pull the camper into New York city, but instead, drop it off at his home, and after the Big Apple experience, pick it up and head back to Jackson.

With the new court ordered desegregation plan in place, I felt that one of my burdens had been lifted, leaving a little more wiggle room and thinking time. From time to time, the idea of job hunting crossed my mind. How would I go about finding another job? Not many jobs, other than the superintendency, paid what I was making. Then too, I was to receive a raise at the end of my first year in the district. I faced quite a dilemma. Asking for a job in another district after only one year in my current position could cause flags of caution to wave. Yet, another year in Jackson would mean even more vicious attacks from my so-called professional colleagues who were determined to rid the central office of this outside change agent. Acting Superintendent, Al Russell, had been nice and supportive, at least when he had time to notice me. Would Russell be appointed superintendent, or would someone outside the district replace him? I had heard that the Board was conducting a nationwide search for a superintendent. A rumor, one day, was that an applicant was in town and had been seen in the central office. I wondered what the future held for me in Jackson.

Meanwhile, Ricky completed his final year of high school and received his diploma in the coliseum where all of the graduation ceremonies were held. He had chosen to attend the University of Alabama with several of his friends from Tuscumbia who had had spent 10 years in school together. His heart was set on obtaining a major in journalism. His decision to attend an out of state institution added to the financial problems for the family. Paying in-state college expenses would be a strain, but with out-of-state tuition added, our budget would have to be tightened even more.

Unexpected Visit

Seated in my office, trying to catch up on long overdue paper work, I was surprised when Belon Winston, the newly appointed black board member walked in and perched himself on a small table on the opposite side of the office and began talking. I reasoned that he wanted to get acquainted with some of the administrators. He began asking questions, most of them general in nature. Eventually, they touched gently upon race and relationships, particularly how I viewed the new desegregation plan. After some 30 minutes, Winston said he enjoyed getting to know me, and walked out.

Bolt from the Blue

With July 5 only one week away, we were already loading the camper and making final plans for our long anticipated vacation. We would leave on Friday after work, go to Wanda's parents for the weekend, and then on Monday, we would head north.

The Tuesday before vacation, I received a call at my office from Dr. V.M. Burkett, Superintendent of Schools in Huntsville, Alabama, a district similar in size to Jackson but more stable, and located within 60 miles of where Wanda and I were reared. The Superintendent wanted to know if I would be interested in becoming his Deputy Superintendent. I could hardly believe what my ears were hearing. The shock was so great that the receiver began shaking in my hand. Trying to remain calm I replied that I would certainly like to talk with him about the position.

"When can you come for an interview?" Dr. Burkett asked.

"How about next Monday?" I quizzed. "We're leaving for vacation this weekend and will be coming through Huntsville that day." And with the time set, I could hardly contain myself. "Unbelievable!" I said as I shared the good news with Wanda, who may have been happier with the information than I.

"This is just great," she exclaimed. "What are your chances of you getting the job?" Wanda wanted to know.

"Personally, I think it's a done deal" I responded with assurance.

Chapter 6

The Shock

All weekend, I dreamed of moving back to Alabama where I would serve as Deputy Superintendent of Huntsville City Schools, a large but rather tranquil school district. Monday at 10:00 a.m., sharp, I arrived for the interview. The Board Members were cordial and allowed the Superintendent, Dr. Burkett, a small, stern, man who had grown up in the district, to pose most of the questions. The entire process was an enjoyable experience, and even though no verbal commitment was made during the interview, I could not imagine being turned down for the job.

When the interview ended, the Superintendent called me aside. "We'll have a board meeting tomorrow night so call me Wednesday morning and I'll let you know the results. I think it went well," he said as he turned to rejoin the Board.

The drive to Williamsburg, with intermittent stops, was long but pleasant. We found a campground near the historic town and spent the night.

Early Wednesday morning we bought tickets for a tour, watched the background and introductory film, and then prepared to enjoy the old town. "I think I'll call and see what the Board decided," I ventured.

I placed the call to hear, "It was unanimous. Welcome aboard! When can you report for duty?" the Superintendent inquired.

"August 1," came my quick response. And so the deal was closed. A relief came over me that was unexplainable. I could never have wished for anything better. It was as if I had been rescued from death row.

The family enjoyed Williamsburg, and then we decided to head for Charlottesville and visit Monticello, a place Ricky had studied about and anxiously waited to view the historic home in person. Just outside Charlottesville we found a rustic campground where, during the evening, we sat around a small open campfire and roasted wieners and marshmallows. The evening was one of the most relaxing times I could remember. After a good night's sleep, the family showered, dressed and were ready to go into the city when I saw a pay phone nearby and decided to call Bob Ross, Board Chairman in Jackson, to let him know I had accepted a new position and would be resigning, effective at the end of July.

I dialed slowly. I could hear the repeated rings and was about to hang up when a gravelly, voice said, "Hello."

"Mr. Ross, this is Brandon Sparkman. I'm calling to let you know that I've accepted a job in another district and will submit my resignation when we return from vacation on the 19th."

Almost shouting, Ross responded, "Doctor, you can't resign. The Board met night before last and named you Superintendent of the Jackson Schools."

Totally stunned, I stood silently unable to think. Finally, I recovered enough to say, "Mr. Ross, this is the greatest shock of my life. I can't even respond. I'll have to think about it a day or two, and then I'll call you."

"Well, give me a call as soon as you can, but we've already decided we want you for our Superintendent," he concluded.

Reeling from the news and in a total state of disbelief, I felt as if an evil force were dragging me back on to death row. I didn't want to think about it. I didn't want to tell the family about the agonizing decision facing us.

"What did he say?" Wanda inquired while the children listened intently.

"You're not going to believe this," I said, shaking my head that was bowed low. "He said the Board met and named me Superintendent. Can you believe that?" I asked. I now had company with which to share my shock and confusion.

After pondering the situation a couple of minutes, Wanda asked, "Did you tell him you would take it?"

"No. I told him I'd call him in a day or two and talk. I was so shocked I couldn't respond. I don't know if I even want to consider staying in Jackson. I've been so pleased that we were leaving. I've just got to think," I said while continuing to shake my head. While my brain said. "Don't even consider the offer", there was that same strange urging I had felt before going to Jackson, telling me to stay in Jackson.

Ricky, Rita and Robert examined every nook and cranny of Monticello, hustling from place to place at a pace that was draining energy rapidly from Wanda and me. The three absorbing minds at work normally would have consumed my attention, giving me an air of excitement also, but this was not a normal time.

A Tough Decision

That evening, Wanda and I went for a walk that lasted more than an hour. We talked about one thing: the job offer. Why should we change plans that had the entire family so excited? The children would be in a fine school system and we would be living near our parents and kin where they could experience close family relationships. Obviously, the superintendent position would be a promotion that could lead to high-level positions and be financially rewarding. But the job would be all-consuming, leaving less time for the family. Certainly there were instructional and staff needs in the Jackson schools that, with my absence, would likely go unmet for a much longer time and the district needed strong direction. I knew what was needed, but with the opposition I would face, could I do the job? What did the family want to do?

That night I slept little. The key point for me was, "Did I have the courage to do whatever it would take to rescue the Jackson Schools?" People would have to be hurt, and I had never had a desire to hurt anyone. The inbred staff had already dug in and was prepared to fight any outsider who was appointed superintendent.

Interim Superintendent Russell had neither made serious decisions nor established a direction for the district even though the district remained in turmoil. Perhaps the title "Interim Superintendent" implied that he was expected only to hold things together until the Board named a new superintendent. Or, maybe his age coupled with his observation of the struggles of two former superintendents had a deterring effect on his willingness to deal with the tough issues. Whatever the case, the Jackson schools were afloat, and the majority of citizens believed it was headed for a certain death.

I wondered if I had the wisdom, stamina and courage to take up the fight that had defeated three good men. Could I make highly unpopular decisions and even dismiss those who refused to support new directions?

I thought I knew what had to be done to pluck the schools from the quagmire, but was unsure if I had the sheer gritty guts to see it through.

Morning came as bright as one could hope for, but nothing had shed light on my quandary. We packed and hit the trail toward the nation's capital. In spite of the natural beauty and newness of the area, minds and discussions could seldom stray from the dilemma we faced. After finding a campground outside D.C. and setting up for the night, I grilled burgers for dinner. Later, Wanda and I took a stroll where we could talk in private. The same questions as before were foremost on our minds with little that had been resolved. As we talked, three considerations seemed to move to center stage. Where could I serve best? Could I cope with the demands of the Jackson job? And what effect would the decision have on the family?

Some Questions Resolved

Wanda assured me that she and the children would be fine, assuming that Robert had a reasonably good teacher in second grade. In spite of warnings about Robert's lack of achievement, his final report card showed that he had been promoted to the next grade. Ricky would be entering college in the fall, and Rita would be in the same high school that Ricky had attended the previous school year. A review of her record with a counselor told her that one more regular school year, plus summer school, would enable her to graduate a year early. Even though she was unhappy that many of her friends from the single grade school she had attended would be enrolled in other schools, she would do well, Wanda assured me. "We'll be OK," she said.

There was no question about where I was needed most. If I could handle the job amid all the conflict and dogged resistance, I was sure I could establish a direction for the rudderless district. I had successfully stood my ground on more than one occasion, and despite formidable opposition and constant harassment, my work had resulted in noticeable progress. Even though I would feel much more comfortable serving as Deputy Superintendent in Huntsville, the greater need was in Jackson.

The question that remained unanswered at this point was, "Could I summons the courage to do whatever would be required to transform the attitude of the staff and move the school system in a positive direction?" To resolve this dilemma, I would have to have some serious discussions with myself—and that I did.

That night, I seemed unable to close my eyes. I tossed and turned while that gnawing question of courage kept demanding an answer. Sometime after midnight, I assured myself that, should I decide to accept the superintendency, I could, and would, do whatever was necessary, hurtful or not, that was in the best interest of the students and the community. Immediately I turned on my side and drifted into a deep sleep.

The next morning I called Bob Ross. "Mr. Ross," I said, "I've thought about the superintendent position and I'm not sure what I'll do. But, if you would like, when we get to New York City day after tomorrow, and I have the family settled in a hotel, I'll catch a plane to Jackson and talk with the Board. But I can't assure you that I will accept the job."

The reply was loud and emphatic. "Doctor, I'll be in my office any time you want to talk with me." His message was clear: "I am the Board."

My response was equally clear, "Mr. Ross, you didn't understand what I said. I said the Board, and every damn member on the Board will be present if I talk."

Bob Ross, a much revered and feared individual, had never before had any educator demand anything of him. After a slight hesitation Mr. Ross said, "Well Helen is out of town, so I'll have to try to get in touch with her. Call me back tomorrow morning. I'll have the meeting set up and can tell you the time and place."

Chapter 7

New Direction for Jackson

I arrived at the airport in Jackson, rented a car and pointed it north toward the office of board member, Joel Amos. When I arrived, all members were seated in a semicircle with the only vacant chair facing them. So, after exchanging greetings and handshakes, I took the empty seat.

Bob Ross proceeded by telling me that I had been elected unanimously to the Superintendency. I would have a one-year contract at a salary of $25,000 plus $250 per month car allowance. He made a few other comments, giving me a chance to gather my thoughts.

When the time was right, I said, "I wouldn't consider accepting a one year contract."

Ross said, "Well Doctor, no superintendent in Jackson has ever had a contract for more than one year, and every one of them stayed as long as they wanted to."

"No sir," I replied. "Dr. Vest didn't stay as long as he wanted to. He was forced to leave, and the central office staff played a major role in that. If I have a one-year contract, they'll run me out also, but if I have a three-year contract, they'll know in advance that they'll have to work long and hard to force me out."

Henry Long, Vice-President of the board, responded: "That makes a lot of sense. I recommend that we give him a contract for three years." And with no further discussion the five members agreed.

Henry was of medium size build, in his 60's, a highly respected, community-minded, man who perhaps unknowingly followed John Wesley's advice, (the man who was the father of the Methodist Church), when he said, "Make as much as you can, save as much as you can, and

72

give as much as you can." Long had established at least two orphans homes and that was just a tip of his contributions to mankind.

"Now, the salary you have offered me is less than $4,000 more than I would make as Assistant Superintendent if I stayed here. That's not enough," I assured them.

"OK," said Ross, "we'll give you $27,000." I nodded. "Does that settle it?" Ross asked.

"I'll take the job," I responded.

With that statement, Bob Ross bounced to his feet and stepped in front of me. I stood also. Pointing his finger in my face and in a demanding voice said, "Doctor, we have just hired you to run the Jackson Public Schools. You'd better be careful what you ask for because you're going to get it. Everybody makes a few mistakes and we'll allow you to make a few, but if you make too many we'll start looking for another superintendent."

I had my directions. Although I didn't know it at the time, these were words I could count on and live by as long as I was in Jackson.

Flight Back to New York for Family

On the plane back to New York, I began to ask myself the question, "Why me? Why'd the Board decide I was the one for the job?" I recalled hearing that the Board was conducting a nationwide search, as well as the rumor that more than one candidate was seen in the central office being escorted by a board member. But I had never been interviewed, and no one had suggested that I was being considered for the position. Or maybe Belon Winston's visit to my office was an informal interview from a black perspective.

Probing over the years, even after I left Jackson, not one Board Member would ever discuss details of my appointment. Questions about why I was considered for the position went unanswered as well.

It seems that the Board had contracted with a consultant to find three outstanding candidates for the position that he could recommend. Immediately after being employed, the consultant hired someone to assist him in this endeavor, and then left for an extended overseas vacation. Although I was totally unaware of it, the second person in the chain just happened to be Dr. Joe Richardson, someone whom I had often used as a consultant during the past six years and was currently the lead consultant in Jackson. While members of the Board were questioning Dr. Richardson about the qualifications of candidates, he told them that someone already on the staff could possibly be the person best suited for the job. When quizzed about his statement, Willis commented on my background and experiences. Additionally, the Board, in all probability, had been informed that I had negotiated the settlement of the elementary desegregation plan with Justin Cohen, which was no small achievement. The Board may have filed that information away in its mind, and not being overly impressed with any of the candidates interviewed, were in a holding pattern. When I called to resign, the Board President, possibly, made an instant decision to go with me: a decision he later sold to other members. Or maybe they did meet and name me Superintendent.

However, there were more important things for me to think about than why I was about to assume the Superintendency of the Jackson Municipal Separate School District. I changed planes in Atlanta and while waiting for my flight I called Wanda. "I accepted the job," I told her. "Take the family to a play because I won't be there in time to go, and we'll be leaving for Jackson in the morning."

The next morning, having experienced little of the city, we packed up for our long trip home. We had to go via Pennsylvania to get our camper. And then with one night spent in a motel enroute, we started the last leg of the drive home. I spent little time in conversation due to a mind that was occupied with the challenging adjustments that lay ahead.

These Were Tough Times

"Vandalism Costs Triple in Jackson Schools"; "ROTC and Voc Ed Moved to Ghetto School"; "School Tensions Spread"; "Walkout Follows Black-Week Observance"; "Unrest Continues"; "White Student's Leg Broken"; "Negro Students Protest with Walkout"; "Embattled Parents Given Encouragement"; "Supreme Court Upholds Bussing, Race Ratios"; "Southern Senator Seeks Nationwide Mixing"; "Councils Attack Mixing Decision"; "Senate Nixes Suburban Mix Plan"; "Senate Votes Funds to Help Mix Schools"; "Mixers Dissatisfied Despite Massive Integration in South"; "Fights Shut Jackson School"; "Jackson Schools Worried By Order"; . . .

These newspaper headlines characterize the mood of the time and the problematic conditions I was about to inherit. Indeed these were troubled times. I hadn't asked for the job but for some unexplainable reason I had it. Now the question was, "How was I going to handle it?" I had never been one to back away from tough situations, and this was no exception.

Responding to a comment made years earlier by a friend who said she admired my courage, Wanda replied, "That's one thing he's never been short on." Like a bronco buster, I would climb into the saddle, spur lightly and hang on until the opposition was subdued. Or could I?

Planning For Transition

Once in Jackson, I called Hilda Lankford, who lived nearby, and asked her to come to our home, and to plan to spend some time there every evening and weekend. Hilda was the one person in Jackson I felt I could confide in. The two of us would spend numerous hours together during off-duty time for the next few days planning for the transition.

I knew that the administrative staff would be geared up to go after me with a passion as soon as the announcement of my appointment was made. They wouldn't adopt a blatant approach but instead would be more devious in order to conceal their motives. Most central office administrators had been in the system for years and the Assistant Superintendents had much seniority at the headquarters. They knew their jobs well and could coast while jabbing and punching undercover as I was attempting to figure out my role and how to handle the hot-button issues I would face. How could I counter their attack, or better still, how could I out-maneuver them and prevent their subterfuge? And a plan began to take shape in my mind.

While I felt that Al Russell would be supportive, I didn't want him as my Administrative Assistant; therefore, I decided to transfer him to Personnel as Assistant Superintendent over that operation. The situation was different for Walter Riley. He had been persistent in his efforts to make me look bad and hinder my work, so he would be reassigned to a new position, Assistant Superintendent for Communication. Presently, no one was responsible for communicating with the media and the community. Walter was good with words and writing, so he would be given a new assignment he'd have to learn while I was learning my job. Then too, since Walter would no longer be in charge of instruction, he would not be undermining the change process in that area.

Wilma Holland had been a problem by hanging on to the status quo and participating in Walter's efforts to railroad me. With this information in mind, I decided that Wilma could be an asset as an elementary school principal, a position from which she had been elevated a year earlier. From the principalship she would not be in a position to block my system-wide programs, and could probably be nursed along into accepting the new direction in her school. Basically, she was a fine, intelligent person following the wrong leadership.

Lawson McCreary, Director of Secondary Schools, was a solid administrator who was loyal and supportive of the person for whom he worked. With new direction and a new boss, I felt confident that I could depend upon Lawson to acquire a positive attitude and direction and to help me carry out my program. Lawson would retain his current position, at least for the time being.

Sandra Wells had served well as Assistant Director of Personnel. While an undying loyalist of Dr. Harry Prince, she was in no position to oppose my initiatives and had always been cooperative with me. I saw no reason to move Sandra.

Then there was Sam Arnold and Jim Minor; both Prince admirers who were not about to switch loyalties to anyone other than another Prince Protégé. While both were in positions to undermine indirectly, their only means of hurting the instructional program would be through delaying tactics. As they had done in the past, they could still use their influence both with the staff and in the community to demoralize and undermine. Sam's influence was much greater than that of Jim because of his control over the purse strings. I already knew that Jim's intimidating behavior was nothing more than a façade. From the top position, I knew I could handle him, so I decided to leave him in that position. As far as Sam, I was unsure of how best to deal with him. He held a critical position and I knew of no one on the staff who could move to that position and immediately manage it effectively in the current crisis. Neither could I visualize Sam in any other position that I could justify creating just to remove his control from over the district's money. His power with the principals through financial control worried me, but I decided to leave him in his position anyway.

Johnny Wise had run the black schools for a number of years before taking over federal programs. During those years of overseeing the schools, he had done a creditable job of organizing instruction and bringing it out of a state of almost total chaos. The Jackson Schools had never had a black assistant superintendent and I planned for Johnny to be the first.

That would be a very positive move with the black community and would offend few if any of the staff. Johnny Wise would be elevated to Assistant Superintendent for Programs.

Since I would no longer be directly over staff development, that responsibility would be moved to the Department of Programs to be overseen by Wise. Additionally, Hilda would be named Director of Staff Development and would work for Wise. As part of her job, she would oversee the large federal grant, except that the financial accounting would be done in the Finance Department with Johnny Wise authorizing the use and release of funds.

With personnel decisions made and reduced to paper, I turned my attention to arranging, in my mind, how I would handle the announcement of my appointment and my pronouncement of reassignment of top administrators. Hilda had assisted me in thinking through implementation ideas to this point, but from here, I would go it alone.

Each morning, I reported for duty on my regular job, never once changing routines or failing to follow through on active projects. The same could be said for Hilda. Not one hint was given that either was aware of any impending events out of the ordinary.

Chapter 8

An Era of Change

At 8:00 a.m. on August 20, 1971, roughly a year from the time I began work as Assistant Superintendent for Personnel and Staff Development, the entire central office administrative staff was notified that Board Chairman, Bob Ross, had called a meeting for 10:00 o'clock in the board room. Also invited were the Principals of the district. Immediately, the office was abuzz with staff members wondering who their new boss would be. Not a single name could be projected, yet all were sure that the purpose of the called meeting was to make that momentous announcement. I walked into the boardroom and took a vacant aisle seat beside Walter Riley. As soon as I was seated, Walter turned to me and said, "I'm certain Mr. Ross is going to introduce the new Superintendent. Who do you think it will be?"

I gestured a, "Don't know", with my hands.

At 10:00 sharp, the heavy steps of Bob Ross could be heard as he walked down the hallway; then complete silence entombed the boardroom as he entered. The rhythm of his steps continued until he reached the front of the room and almost in military style made one left turn and then another that brought him face to face with his audience. Without hesitating or prefacing his announcement, he began, "I'm here to announce that Dr. Brandon Sparkman is your new Superintendent. Dr. Sparkman!" He motioned for me to come forward, and without further comment he swiftly departed. Not one sound could be heard other than the footsteps of Bob Ross as he left the scene.

I slid out of my chair, walked briskly to the podium and looked at the audience. Never before had I seen so many blood-drained faces, furrowed deeply with worry and disbelief. I had visualized exactly that which I was now seeing. Many of those seated before me were the ones who had almost succeeded in getting me out of Jackson. What other demeanor could they possibly exhibit now?

"There's no longer room for discrimination in the Jackson Public Schools," I began. "Anyone found discriminating will be dismissed. The purpose of schools is to educate children and youth regardless of race, color or creed, and that's exactly what we're going to do. Starting now, instruction will be first priority in everything we do, and we **will** develop a fine program for all of our students. This feat will require dedication and teamwork. If you can't be a team member you had better leave right now because if you refuse, you'll be fired. We'll work together for the betterment of everyone, and we'll build a system that will make all of us proud. From this point forward, we'll no longer be living in the past, but will be building a vision for a better tomorrow. I'm honored to be your Superintendent and look forward to working with you." And having spoken words never before heard in Mississippi, I concluded with, "You're dismissed."

Those words brought about the most significant changes that Jackson's schools had ever known. No foot dragging would be permitted. They could no longer try to keep desegregation from working in order to reverse it, as some administrators had inferred. Blacks and whites would work as a team for the benefit of all. And optimism and cooperation would be expected.

Fireworks Begin

I left the boardroom and went to the superintendent's outer office. Before I could say a word, Ruth Holloway, who had been Secretary to the Superintendent for several decades, met me at the door and said, "Dr. Sparkman, I plan to retire at the end of this week!"

Very much surprised, I asked her to stay on, at least for a while, but she declined saying she had planned to retire earlier but promised to stay as long as Dr. Russell was in office. Well, that was that, so I would have to deal with that loss almost immediately.

I walked on into the Superintendent's office where I found that Al Russell had already vacated the office. Immediately, there was a buzz indicating someone wanted to speak with me. With a degree of uncertainty,

I picked up the receiver to hear Ruth Holloway announce that I had a caller on the line. The push of a button and a "Hello," got me an earful.

"I'm going to sue every SOB in that central office," a bellicose voice roared. Without thinking, I responded, "You have every right to do so. That's what the courts are for. If you decide to proceed, just call our attorney Artie Ulmus. Goodbye."

Two other things of significance occurred that afternoon. First was a phone call from the program chairman of the Jackson Rotary Club asking if I would speak to the group on Thursday? I gave an affirmative answer, recalling that I had spoken to civic clubs on numerous occasions. Having been a member and president of a club, I generally was aware of how these clubs function and their expectations of speakers. Those with which I was familiar had from 25 to 50 members and wanted a speaker to show up, speak up, and shut up after no more than 15 or 20 minutes. I knew that my preparation time would be very limited, but I was sure that I could pull something together that would be appropriate.

The second major event was an in-person contact by a radio call-in host who wanted me to be a guest on his show on Friday. I offered every excuse I could corral, but none of them worked. Finally I caved in and accepted my first, and last such appearance.

I asked Mrs. Holloway to have Hilda come to my office. When I told Hilda that Mrs. Holloway was leaving at the end of the week, she said, "I have just the person for you."

"Who?" I inquired.

"Beth Noles, my secretary," she responded. As my mouth flew open, Hilda said, "I know you don't know her well, but she is marvelous. She can do everything you will want and will do it better than anyone you will ever find. I know you have a secretary, but she'll not be able to do that job well. Beth can, and furthermore, she will be totally loyal to you. Who else can you move in that you can always count on for loyalty?" I had to admit that her suggestion made sense.

"I'll talk with her tomorrow," I said.

The remainder of the afternoon and early evening was spent planning for a staff meeting I intended to call the next morning. There was sure to be some unhappy people after the meeting, but there would be a smile or two also.

Changes and Direction for Central Office

Early Tuesday morning I asked my secretary to notify the Assistant Superintendents, Inservice Assistant, and all directors to report to the boardroom at 9:00 for a staff meeting. When I entered, I found everyone present and silent as a few nervous smiles greeted me. Some of those present expected to be notified of dismissal because of previous behavior. They would be happy to know that they still had a job—just any job.

"There's going to be some reorganization, or reshuffling, of staff that will be effective tomorrow. But first, I want to talk about some changes I want in the way the central office and staff functions. Many, many times I've seen strangers enter this building not knowing how to find the office, or person, they were looking for. Since the Personnel Office is the most obvious one, they went there and sometimes stood for 10 minutes while being ignored. That has to stop. When people enter this building, I want them greeted with a smile and an offer of help. We need to cultivate all the friendships we can."

"The next problem I want solved is this. Many times I have called different offices only to listen to the phone ring until I gave up. This doesn't happen to me only. That too has to stop. When anyone calls the central office I want the phone answered before the third ring. Now, I know that people have to leave their offices for various reasons, so here's what I want done. Jim, I want a desk set up out there near the main entrance. I also want at least four comfortable chairs nearby and a coffee pot. The desk is to have a phone system that will serve as an extension for every phone in the building. On the third ring of any phone, the person serving as receptionist will answer to give information and to take messages. My Secretary, Helen Morrow will man that desk. With her great smile and bubbly personality, she is a natural for that position. I want the central office to be a friendly, inviting place that gives every caller, whether by phone or in person, the impression that the Jackson School System is here to serve people and to do it well."

Immediately, Sam cut in, "We don't have any money in the budget for such a phone system as you have described. That will not be cheap."

"Find the money," I responded.

"You're calling the shots," Sam stated emphatically.

"You bet," was the closing statement on that issue.

"We have no one with exclusive responsibility for preparing press releases, dealing with the media, and coordinating communications with the community. One of our greatest problems revolves around 'image.' Success in any endeavor requires a positive image, and we sure fall short in this regard. Therefore, I am creating a position called Assistant Superintendent for Communications and am assigning Walter to that position. He has good writing and communication skills and will be a natural for the position. Of course, Walter, you will work closely with my office." Walter Riley nodded and breathed a sigh of relief.

"Johnny Wise will fill the position that will be vacated by Walter, and it will carry the title of Assistant Superintendent for Programs," I continued. Johnny almost fell from his chair. (*Joking later, some who observed him closely said that with that assignment, Johnny was the closest to being white he would ever be.*) Johnny Wise would be the first black person to occupy an office of Assistant Superintendent in the Jackson Public Schools. "Hilda will be moved from the Personnel office to the office of Programs to work with Johnny serving as Director of Staff Development."

While people were congratulating Johnny and Hilda on their promotions, Wilma Holland said, "I'd like to stay as close to the students as I can." With that statement, I said, "Good. I'm assigning you to an Elementary Principal position. And finally, Al will move into my office where he will serve as Assistant Superintendent for Personnel."

"For the time being, all others will retain current assignments. I expect nothing less than total support in our efforts to restructure the district and put a new face on it. We're through fighting. We're going to move forward as a team with instruction as our focus. If you can't make a contribution toward an improved instructional program, regardless of your position, you won't deserve your position and I can assure you that it'll quickly become endangered." I dismissed the staff but asked Mike Israel to stay.

"Mike," I began, "the data that you provide with the computer is virtually worthless. There are so many errors that every department either uses it reluctantly or outright refuses to use it. Accounting, by every measure, should be on computer, but you and your staff make so many mistakes that Mr. Stoddard refuses to even consider involving you. That's got to change or we're going to close down the operation"

Mike shifted in his chair nervously and responded, "Just give me a little time and we'll take care of it."

"Mike, you have had lots of time. It's now time to stop making excuses and get the job done or get out!" I warned.

"Yes sir, I'll take care of it."

After the meeting I sent for Beth Noles. After a few minutes of friendly chitchat, I got to the point. "Mrs. Holloway is retiring effective Friday afternoon and I want you to replace her as my Secretary."

"Well now, Dr. Sparkman, I don't know if I can do that job. I think you'd better get somebody else."

"No, I want you in that position and I'm sure you can handle it well," I insisted.

"No Sir," Beth pleaded, "I don't think I'm the one for that job."

"Are you certain about that decision?" I queried.

"Yes Sir and I'm sorry. I appreciate your thinking of me," she said while rising from her chair.

Superintendent's Office Staff Finalized

I called Hilda and told her what had happened. "You just wait. I'll talk with her. She can do the job, and I'll see that she changes her mind."

Bob Ross called and suggested that I hire two secretaries to replace Mrs. Holloway. "The Board and our attorney need someone with excellent shorthand skills to take detailed minutes of board meetings and to assist Ulmus with secretarial services in his work on legal matters and board assignments." I agreed and assured the Chairman that I would take care of the matter pronto.

Next morning, Hilda came to my office to report that she had talked with Beth and that she was ready to talk with me again. I sent for her and with Hilda present, told them there would be two secretaries: one for me and one for the Board and its Attorney, with both working together under my direction.

Beth's eyes lit up. She said, "If you will get Sue Ann as the Board Secretary, I'll be glad to work for you." Of course, Sue Ann Wells, whom I rejected early on for my secretary, would now work for me and prove to be superb, and the best at shorthand I had ever known.

Initiation to Media

Thursday shortly before noon, I headed downtown to the Heidelberg Hotel where I was told the Rotary Club would meet. Parking in a nearby lot, I entered the old landmark hotel through the rear entrance. I peeped into the ballroom before proceeding to the front desk for information. Obviously, they were having some kind of large luncheon in that room because there were many tables set up ready to accommodate a multitude.

I inquired about the location of the Rotary meeting, and my heart almost stopped beating when I was told it would be in the ballroom. Having arrived early, I walked slowly toward the ballroom while my stomach churned and my palms sweated. I approached the ballroom door once more, but now it was worse. I noted that the head table was on a platform some four or five feet high and I would be speaking to what looked like maybe four hundred members. As I stood in the door, a TV camera rolled up beside me. While pacing nervously, a second camera was set up inside the room. After a few people came in, I turned to someone standing nearby and asked, "Why are the TV cameras here?"

"Because you're speaking," was the shocking response.

Seated with the club officers high above the audience, I worried that I had spent so little time preparing my remarks. Here was an old country plowboy with time spent in small towns. Now I was about to address the elite of a big city with TV cameras facing me. I would be seen and my speech heard by thousands throughout Jackson and for miles outside the city. What could I say that would be worthy of this attention? If the meal was good, I didn't notice. I was frantically attempting to reorganize my thoughts and modify my speech as those seated on either side talked to me incessantly. Worse still, they often asked questions, which totally destroyed my precious minutes for concentration.

When introduced, I walked to the podium. Looking down on the audience, the people appeared to be a great distance away. I began my talk while blinding lights made my notes useless. One minute after my harried presentation, I would have been hard pressed to recall a single thing I had said, other than the fact that I placed emphasis on the need for an outstanding instructional program. That continued to be my major trademark because, as I contended, instruction was the primary and unremitting purpose of schools.

Someone once said that the best lessons are the ones learned through error. Well, I had just gotten more than a lesson: I had just received an education.

That was my first time to make a speech before a big TV camera, but it wasn't the last. After that maiden voyage, I made few speeches in Jackson that were not televised. The camera crew seemed to follow me everywhere. They were at civic clubs, PTA Council meetings, and even in church sanctuaries where I spoke. But TV was not the only shadow I had. Newspaper reporters were omnipresent. Almost every word I spoke, I was likely to read the next day. I had to be exceedingly careful of the words I used because the wrong word or phrase could fuel an explosion. However, I had to admit that the reporters were fair and the editor was very supportive of the public schools. That, nevertheless, did not stop them from reporting the bad as well as the good. The press was fair, and that was all I could expect.

From Frying Pan into Fire

Seated beside a call-in radio host, microphone inches from mouth, I faced the most unpleasant hour of my entire life. Having grown up on an isolated farm then migrating to small towns, I was unaware of the hatred and vociferous vindictiveness so-called civilized city people were capable of exhibiting. But I learned quickly. Calls kept coming in blasting the Board of Education; wanting to know what I was going to do to stop the "Niggers" from taking over the schools; lambasting the weak-kneed attorney; asking for my plan for reversing the court approved plan; assuring me that the citizens would not support and pay for bussing kids all over Jackson; complaining bitterly about morals, language and behavior of black pupils; and on and on and on. One woman said, "I just want to know what you would say to a black boy who told your daughter he wanted to make her pregnant?"

"I would say the same thing to him that I'd say to a white boy who made the same statement," was my reply.

After about 15 minutes of these horrendous questions and insults, I whispered to the host, "I'm quitting." With a wave of the hand, the host was saying hold on. Time and again at commercial breaks, I, while sweating profusely, repeated my statement, but the host would plead with me to continue.

At the half hour, there was a five minute break. I slammed my headset down and in total disgust said, "I'm through. I'm not going back on." The host begged me to stay, promising that the second half-hour would be better. Eventually, I gave in, agreeing to continue.

A miracle occurred during the break. From that point forward, almost every caller was positive about the Jackson school situation and asked reasonable questions. Of course I would never know what had happened, but my guess was that someone made numerous calls prior to the final round, recruiting friends of the Jackson schools to call the show. Additionally, the person answering the phone lines may have screened the callers carefully before putting them on. Whatever happened, the radio show ended on a positive note. It was over at last. But immediately, I wrote an indelible note on my brain to never accept a similar invitation again.

Washington Connection

As the "call buzz" sounded, I grabbed the receiver, "Yes?"

"Henry Mabry is here to see you," Beth said.

"Send him in," I replied. Henry Mabry was president of a highly respected investment firm and had served with the group that developed the desegregation plan. Although not attending all of the meetings, his suggestions received full focus because he had connections in Washington. In fact, it was said that he was on a first-name basis with President Richard Nixon and had "faced off" with him about school desegregation after the President finished a speech in another southern city. Although rebuffed by the President, Mr. Nixon apparently maintained contact with him and sought his advice on state related matters.

I greeted Mabry warmly and immediately had two cups of coffee brought in from the reception area. After a brief chat, Henry handed me a sheet of paper containing the White House letterhead. On the stationery, someone had written in longhand the name, David Catchen and a telephone number. Henry informed me that Catchen was a member of the President's White house staff and would be my personal contact when I needed anything from Washington. "If you have questions or concerns, or if more federal funds are urgently needed, call David. If you need an appointment with someone in Washington, call David, and when you are in the capital city, go by and talk with him. He will be expecting to hear from you when you need help."

When Mabry departed, I eased myself into my chair and stared in amazement at the name and telephone number beneath the letterhead. I could never have dreamed of having a White House contact when I was breaking my back picking cotton on a tenant farm. Access to the White House by phone, and in person, was unbelievable to me, but it had happened.

Bussing Plan Torpedoed

Busses for carrying out the court approved desegregation plan were ordered early in July and were scheduled for delivery in time for the opening of school on September 6. The addition of 70 busses to the existing fleet would require much time and money. Space for parking the busses; shop facilities for service and maintenance; employment of mechanics and service personnel as well as drivers; establishment of routes and schedules; and arranging for temporary aides and volunteers for assuring order and safety, (a requirement under the court order) were some of the matters to be attended to for expanding the transportation service. The tight timeline placed a tremendous burden on the Director of Transportation but also on other departments, especially Personnel and Finance. The time was far too short but not impossible.

Pupil transportation was just one of many problems dumped on me as I took the reins of the beleaguered school district. The staff was moving along well toward meeting the opening of school deadline for having busses ready to roll. While none of the vehicles would be delivered for almost a month, the Transportation Department was preparing to receive them and get them ready for the road. A grant application was in Washington that included funds for this venture, which was unique to Mississippi. Also included in the request were funds for construction of the northern fifth/sixth grade plaza. Assurances were given that federal funds would be made available to cover these costs.

As if I had not been hammered enough during my first weeks in office, this time, the ax fell. President Nixon announced that no federal funds could be spent for bussing. My heart almost stopped beating. Thoughts of disaster and defeat whirled through my mind. More than $400,000 had been obligated, and there was no money in the ultra-tight budget to take up the slack. How could I deal with this? Refusing to comply with the court order was not a good choice. Cutting $400,000 from other budgeted items would be devastating to the instructional program, an announced priority. A sudden request for additional taxes would totally destroy any confidence and hope the community might have in me. This problem, along with the others, was the reason I tossed and turned in bed each night. Early on, I had trouble deciding which I dreaded most: going to bed each night or going to work each morning.

The next morning I slowly dialed the Washington number that had been handed to me only a few days earlier. With David Catchen on the phone, I presented my dilemma and expressed great disappointment that I had been set up only to be let down. In a calm manner, Catchen assured me that something would be worked out. The White House staff would need time to formulate a solution, but he told me to move forward with my plans. Telling someone to remain calm, and remaining calm when the world is caving in are two different things, and my world was coming unraveled.

There are two forms of panic. One is the type where the individual grows pale, sweats profusely, has irrepressible twitches, and cannot think logically. The second is a controlled type where knots, too large to describe, are rolling unceasingly in the stomach, sometimes producing low level nausea, while the outward appearance deceitfully portrays a calm assurance. Some of my demanding experiences of previous years had enabled me to control my emotions and behavior at times such as this when I really wanted to run. During the next few weeks, this panic-free appearance would serve me and the school district well.

"What are you going to do now?" inquired Sam Arnold as he nodded incessantly. "I could've told you this whole thing wouldn't work," he insisted.

"Everything will be alright," I assured him. "Just keep things moving on track and be ready for the opening of school. That's all you need to be concerned about," came my confidently sounding reply.

"Well I sure hope you know what you're talking about because the money is not here to pay for this entire outlandish program," Sam warned.

"It'll be ok," I assured Sam once more.

Moving Ahead

People were employed, maintenance facilities were enlarged, school attendance zones were redrawn, bus routes and schedules were finalized as if everything were in proper order, and problems were only faint remembrances of the past. But I knew differently. Either it would come together, or at the last minute all hell would break loose. All I could do was keep the faith and calm the troops.

Positive School Opening Imperative

Money for initial construction of one plaza had been requested but denied. That was a problem that would have to be dealt with, but not now. Right now, a smooth opening of school was paramount in my mind. The plaza could be shifted to the back burner temporarily.

Two meetings had been held with the principals and central office administrators jointly for planning and feedback on preparation for the opening of school. Everyone was to be totally alert to conditions, with prevention of problems being foremost, not solutions following problem occurrences. Acceptance, objectivity and courtesy were stressed. But of equal or greater importance, actual instruction must begin almost immediately on opening day. Plans must be made to collect data and organize classes as rapidly as possible then quickly introduce an interesting and provocative lesson. Few problems occur when good teaching in going on. Not only was this procedure expected to be followed on the first day of school, but on every day of school.

I scheduled some time each day during the next week to visit schools. I wanted to be certain that the buildings had an inviting appearance; that plans had been made by each principal that incorporated the ideas discussed during the district meetings; and that indeed schools were ready to receive students. I was pleased with the intensive preparations being made. As I had assured myself, and then the public in my first news release, instruction was receiving attention, even before the opening of school.

Budget Presented to Mayor and Council

Traditionally, the school district budget was presented to the Jackson City Council the last week in August. In preparing the budget, Sam had written an unprecedented preface that reflected his philosophy pertaining to the changes taking place in the schools. In this preface, he also listed all new positions added for the new school year; the ones he had strenuously opposed because, as he said many times, "There are no funds available to cover these positions."

I first received the budget from Sam the day before it was to be presented to the Council. Surprised by the initial content, I demanded that the extraordinary additions be deleted, keeping it in line with previous budget documents. Sam had already had copies of the budget printed and contended that it was too late to make changes.

"Your philosophy, as well as the list of new positions **will be deleted**," I ordered with visible authority.

The Board had approved a budget that left the tax rate unchanged, even though it had the option of raising or lowering taxes. Bob Ross, Sam and I met with the Mayor and City Council to present the budget for its information and blessing. With some disparaging remarks and venomous statements by one Council member about that which was happening in the schools, and with some supportive notes by other members, the budget was accepted.

Mayor Richard Miles had written a letter to me congratulating me on my appointment to the Superintendency and offering his support, but we had not met in person prior to the budget review. After the meeting, Mayor Miles walked up to me, shook my hand and said, "Doctor, I don't know if you drink or not, but if you don't, you may need to start. This job is likely to require it."

Federal Funds Received

The Jackson School District received the expected federal grant on Friday, August 27. Slightly more than $2,000,000 was approved, but the joker was that none of it could be used for bussing. The grant was the second largest award in America for desegregation and consumed almost two-thirds of all the funds allocated to Mississippi schools. But none of it could be used to save the district from what looked like a catastrophe. Well thanks a lot!

I called David Catchen. "What in the world are we going to do?" I asked.

David responded, "You have to buy supplies, furniture and equipment out of your general fund, don't you?"

"Sure," I answered.

"Then take that money and pay for the busses and use the grant funds to buy the items you would normally pay for from the general fund. Think you can handle that?" he asked.

I thanked him and headed to Sam's office. Sam indicated that handling the bus expenditure this way would take a little maneuvering but he could work it out.

Chamber Support or Nonsupport?

The power structure of Jackson was concerned about the economic well-being and future of the city. Business had dropped, housing starts were near zero, people were moving out of the city, and new industries being sought by Jackson were locating elsewhere. The fact that good public schools were necessary to the well-being of Jackson was rapidly becoming apparent.

The Chamber of Commerce and a few progressive organizations came forward with statements of support for the public schools. Some of the merchants and businessmen formed an Education Task Force and hired a director with funds which they donated. They began to say, "We don't just want good public schools, we are going to have them. We don't care what it takes to make our schools good; we will do what it takes and will see that our school officials take the necessary measures to ensure quality."

Jacksonians for Public Education was organized. This group and the Education Task Force were biracial organizations. Community leaders of the two races began to communicate and it soon became apparent that these groups had much more in common than past experiences had indicated to either.

Unsuspected by Chamber leaders, one member acting independently, polled the membership to determine if they supported the Chamber's stand in support of public schools. Some business leaders called a meeting to which the Mayor and I were invited. The basic question was whether the

Chamber should become less vocal in support of the schools until major desegregation issues were settled? After hearing several negative remarks and only a couple of positive ones, I was moved to say that from a personal standpoint, the success of Jackson's public schools was unimportant to me. Their success or failure would have little effect on my professional career because when I took the job, most people believed the schools were doomed to fail. I told the group that they were the ones to be concerned. It was they, their families and their businesses that would be affected. To support, or not support, public schools was their decision to make. I pointed out that from a professional standpoint, I was greatly concerned. I stated that the school staff would give them a fine school system if they wanted it and had the courage to lend support.

There were immediate expressions of support, and that support never dwindled as long as I was Superintendent of the Jackson schools.

Schools Off To Good Start

On the day after Labor Day, schools opened in Jackson without a hitch. There were isolated minor complaints during the remainder of the week, but the week was one that made me proud.

Principals and teachers had taken seriously the challenge of having schools and classrooms in tiptop shape and being ready to begin teaching on opening day. Thus, with minor kinks straightened the schools ran rather smoothly once underway.

Most elementary teachers managed their situations rather well even though many were not pleased to be teaching in their assigned schools. Junior high and senior high teachers who had been uprooted from their long-held posts were less happy. Black teachers complained little. After all, it was people of their race who had forced this matter upon the schools. Many found themselves in better situations than they had ever had, except for the fact that they were not comfortable handling discipline problems involving white students. But most principals assumed added responsibility for maintaining proper behavior, even in classrooms. Still, there were a few white students who had been brought up in homes that openly expressed hatred for blacks, and some of these pushed the limits both in classrooms and around the schools.

Most unhappy were white junior and senior high school teachers assigned to ghetto area schools with few white students and a multitude of hard-to-handle students. Yet here too, principals were as supportive as possible. But in some instances, teachers had been transferred from high-achieving, academically oriented schools where misbehavior was rare, and the instructional level far exceeded the norm for that grade. Now these same instructors faced 30 to 40 students in each class, many of whom had never been exposed to the level of expectation these teachers brought with them. Many students were loud, boisterous, and inattentive. This situation produced extreme frustration for both teachers and students. Yet little could be done to right a wrong that had been thrust upon them.

Within a few days, several teachers threw in the towel and resigned, but even those had to be replaced by other white instructors who were ill prepared for the assigned job. I had made clear to everyone during Teacher Institute that my door was open to any who needed me, and a number of teachers, individually, took advantage of this offer. Most of them cried and begged for a transfer, but there was nothing I could do, while abiding by the court order. I sympathized with each one and offered supervisory and consultant assistance. They left my office still greatly troubled but aware that they would receive whatever assistance was available and that there was a sympathetic ear in the central office.

Positive Press

The editorial in the September 9, 1971 edition of the *Boca Raton News* flashed a headline entitled: ***Jackson, of all places***.

>   *Of all unlikely places, Jackson, Mississippi, has come up with a school desegregation plan that is a model in style, if not in detail, for the rest of the nation.*
>
>   *The fact is that Jackson, after eight years of turmoil and court battles, simply wearied of it all and decided to devise something workable.*
>
>   *That was the basic place to start—with a commitment to stop fighting and start building.*
>
>   *School systems everywhere should take note. For instance, Palm Beach County should take note. And Pontiac, Michigan.*
>
>   *The beauty of the Jackson approach is that it does what the Supreme Court really was talking about in the Swan (Charlotte-Mecklenburg) case. It uses imagination and local good will and cooperation. And a few buses, too.*

> *Thus Jackson has a new hope for its school system, desegregation and all.*
> *It may not be perfect. In fact, it may ultimately fail. But for a while, at*
> *least, Jackson, Mississippi, of all places, has set a style.*[2]

The Bomb

Spurred on by observations and assurance that things were in good shape, I began to shed some of my anxiety overload. I suggested that the family plan to spend the weekend visiting both our parents, some 300 miles away. With everything still looking good at noon Friday of the first week of school, I told Wanda to get the kids ready for the trip as soon as they arrived from school, and I would be home by 4:00 p.m.

As we headed north, I said to the family that this was the first time since receiving the job offer that I had been able to relax. Just being with the family for several hours while everyone was awake was a treat to me. The trip was pleasant and uneventful, just as I had hoped it would be. When we arrived at our destination, I got the first full night of sleep I could remember. The second night was no different. The family greatly enjoyed the parents and grandparents and was saddened when Sunday noon arrived with departure time just around the corner.

With two good nights of sleep under my belt, a peaceful weekend and enjoyable conversations with the family, my dread of going to work was fading rapidly. Upon arriving home around 9:00 p.m., as I slid my key into the door lock, I heard the phone ringing. Dashing across the room, I lifted the receiver and gave my usual "Hello."

The male voice at the other end said, "This is TV station WXYZ and I need to know if we are going to have school tomorrow?"

"Sure," I responded.

"You are aware, are you not, that all state funds for the Jackson schools have been cut off by an executive order issued by Governor Williams?" the caller questioned.

After a moment's hesitation, I said, "No, I'm not."

"Well are we still going to have school tomorrow?" he asked.

"You bet we are," came a cool assurance.

The next two hours were spent responding to calls, mostly from radio stations, the other TV stations, and from local and national news

---

[2]   "Jackson of All Places," *Boca Raton News*, (September 9, 1971).

correspondents. Jackson had been prominent in the national news for a long time and tomorrow, as well as the week, would see the name of the city and state in large print in almost every newspaper and magazine in the country. Also growing in size were the knots inside my stomach.

In Court against the Governor

As soon as the Governor's news conference announcing the withholding of funds to the Jackson schools was over, school board attorney Artie Ulmus began work on Saturday preparing a statement concerning Executive Order 87, and how it was directed. He detailed instances in which courts had already ruled that state laws restricting use of funds for bussing must be set aside when districts are ordered to provide transportation as a means of implementing a plan. Information was released stating that bus routes and schools would operate on Monday the same as they had during the previous week.

The School Board, on the following Tuesday, requested the court to free money being withheld by the state. In response, the U.S. District Judge entered an order setting September 27 as the date for a hearing on the Board's petition for a preliminary injunction against withholding of state funds to the Jackson Public Schools.

If there was anything I didn't need, it was another new experience. But the ball was rolling, and it seemed that nothing could stop it. So I went to court as a primary witness against the state of Mississippi. I spent a significant amount of time being examined and cross examined. Never before had I appeared in court, except for truancy hearings while I served as a principal.

One of the state's contentions was that the federal grant received by the Jackson schools prohibited their use for bussing; therefore, the city schools were using state funds for that purpose. The Executive Order was issued pursuant to a state law enacted in 1953 prohibiting transportation of pupils living in, and assigned to schools within municipalities. After hearing both sides, the judge issued a restraining order restoring funds to the Jackson schools.

Tense Times Cause Over Reaction

I received a call from an extremely nervous acting principal who explained that a minor explosion had occurred in the school's basement storage room, but little or no damage had been done. He had notified the police but everything was under control.

The following day a newspaper headline read, "School Bomb Damage Light." The FBI was involved with the local police in the investigation. Investigators reported that the device was a low-order homemade bomb probably using black powder or some similar explosive. They reportedly stated that definite identification of the device would probably take two to three weeks. The damage was limited to minor splintering of a wooden cabinet, the report stated.

Actually, a mischievous student went to the basement where unneeded and discarded items were stored, found an old wooden cabinet, stuck a large firecracker in it, lit the firecracker and quickly departed. These were the kind of things that occurred occasionally when I was a high school student, but the police were never involved, let alone the FBI. But pranksters were allowed less latitude during this time of tension and suspicion.

Classroom Visits to Boost Teachers

I set aside a few hours each week for visiting classrooms. Undaunted by fourteen hundred classrooms, I was determined to show an interest in the instructional program and in those on the front line. I would go to the principal's office, unannounced, and say to the Principal, "Let's visit classrooms." Down the hallway we would go, open a door and I would say, "Hi, I'm Brandon Sparkman. How's it going?" With the brief greeting and a few words, we would move to the next room. Usually, I was able to speak to each teacher in a given school during that one visit. However, a few times I was summoned to my office due to emergency situations requiring my attention. In such cases, I would make a return visit.

Much positive feedback came from the classroom visits. First, it provided teachers an opportunity to meet the Superintendent personally. Second, it reassured teachers of the importance of their role as perceived by the top office. And finally, it alerted principals to the fact that the Superintendent could show up impromptu to take the temperature of the instructional program.

State Teacher Pay Hike Supported

The Hinds County/Jackson Legislative Delegation dispatched representatives of the Jackson members to my office for consultation. They reported that the Legislative Finance Committee had virtually completed its budget recommendations and found they still had funds available. Some had suggested a teacher pay raise while others noting the extremely tight operating budgets of school districts recommended that the funds be used for that purpose. Others were opposed to doing anything to help public education. These gentlemen told me they wanted my recommendation and assured me their delegation had the votes to decide how the funds would be allocated and would follow whatever advice I gave them.

This was a tough question. There were burning needs that somehow had to be met. Money was tight because the Board of Education deliberately avoided raising taxes. This action was taken to avoid further alienation of the public schools. After serious consideration, I said, "Our operating funds are being drained rapidly by the unusual conditions and demands that we face, and may reach a critical point before the fiscal year is finished. On the other hand, the teachers of Mississippi receive the lowest pay of any in the nation, yet are facing the most serious challenges of their careers. They need a morale booster, so I suggest that the money go for salaries."

Then I congratulated members of the delegation for even considering a teacher raise during this time of turmoil. "I don't believe there is another legislature in the South that would take this bold step," I asserted.

Teacher Retraining Program Continues

Visitation to other school districts was no longer needed. The approach to teaching, as previously observed, had been adopted in Jackson and was making steady progress. However, training sessions continued utilizing consultants and volunteer substitutes. When a teacher would complain of having serious problems teaching students, an instructional supervisor, or a consultant would be sent to assist. This immediate help, along with the Superintendent's visits, tended to boost morale considerably.

Racial Bias Confronted

With two exceptions, principals were careful to avoid behaviors that would indicate racial prejudice. One white principal was accused of giving preferential treatment to white students. The other, a black principal, was accused of being rude and threatening to both white students and parents. The instances cited in both cases, and the people reporting the actions, made it clear that neither principal was colorblind in dealing with people of the opposite race.

I arranged a conference with the white principal, during which I confronted him with information I had gathered. The principal denied the accusations, but assured me that he would take special precautions in the future to avoid any appearance of discrimination. With that assurance, I warned him and sent him on his way.

The black principal came to my office upon request. When approached about accusations, he became hostile: not just defensive. His pent up anger gushed forth, and he showed no inclination to change his attitude or behavior. I warned him and sent him back to the school.

The next day, I invited Justin Cohen to my office. This was the first time Cohen had been in the Superintendent's office. While we had coffee, I reported to Cohen the accusations against the Principal and described the Principal's response. Justin assured me that he would handle the matter himself. I never received another complaint about either principal.

Special Board Meeting

The CEO of a New York firm came to Jackson to sell me on an Instructional program purported to be highly effective in helping students learn the social sciences, kindergarten through grade nine. I was impressed with the instructional approach and the material. But, the price far exceeded anything I had ever spent on a new instructional program. I told the CEO that I would consider purchasing the program, but would have to consult with the staff before making a decision.

Later, I decided to invite the gentleman from New York back to Jackson to present his program to the Board of Education. I felt highly uncomfortable making a purchase of this magnitude without Board involvement.

A special meeting of the Board was called and some one and a half hours were spent in hearing the presentation. Without any discussion, Bob Ross said, "We'll take this matter under advisement. The meeting is adjourned."

As soon as I shook the hand of the visitor, Mr. Ross motioned for me to accompany him outside. He turned to me and said. "Doctor, we hired you to tell us what you need. The Board is made up of busy people and we don't have time to spend helping you decide what to do. You make the decisions and inform us. Don't ask us: tell us."

I had to hear the same message twice to totally understand. I had been hired to run the Jackson schools. I vowed never to make that mistake again. There would be times when board members could have prevented me from getting burned, but they let me learn from the pain. Years later, I longed for such a board of education.

Chapter 9

Battles for Control

Most state capitol cities attract just about every special interest and pressure group in existence. It is in these cities that fanatical groups find large and diverse populations, but also available are substantial amounts of information, as well as more accessibility to sources of power and money. Jackson was no exception.

Segregationist Holdouts

The hardcore segregationists had pretty well lost their identity. The back of the Klan had been broken and was rudderless, yet from time to time some members, or former members, would foment minor problems that had to be countered. The black community would become infuriated over the slightest incident that bore the markings of segregationists or the Klan. These segregation conspirators would love to disrupt or destroy the public schools, so the staff and I constantly had to guard against their activities and be prepared to reassure blacks that their efforts would bear no fruit. Another factor that worked against the segregationists was the stance of the white power structure. With its new direction, the troublemakers would receive no support from the very ones that formerly had urged them on.

Black Militants

Then there were the black militants whose primary goal was to provoke distrust among their people. Their delight was in finding something to complain about regardless of lack of severity of the matter. Any sign of suspected Klan-induced activity resulted in a response that required days or weeks of damage control measures.

Friends of Public Education

Citizens for Public Education was an organization with purity of motive but unrealistic in some of its approaches. Members of this group tended to think that they could quickly and easily convert the thinking and attitude of the average Jacksonian to their more liberal makeup. To do this, the group was determined to become the communications agency for the Jackson Public Schools. Some within the group attempted to dominate or control Walter Riley and his staff, or else replace the Office of Communications with their own communications network, and to speak on behalf of the district. Eventually, convinced that I would not equivocate or relent, they accepted a supportive role in which the Office of Communications would determine helpful activities that the organization could handle well and call on it for support. After months of misdirected efforts and damage, the leadership joined forces with the district and was helpful in creating a more positive image of the Jackson Public Schools.

HEW

As if school districts wrestling with court ordered desegregation didn't have enough problems, the U.S. Department of Health, Education and Welfare (HEW) awarded grants to militant and activist groups to cause trouble. These grants supported efforts to teach black students their rights. But, it didn't stop there. These students were trained to apply confrontational tactics to determine if their rights would be violated.

Initially, school officials were unaware of the cause of an occasional incident involving unruly and boisterous behavior that appeared to be unprovoked. As these episodes occurred more often, an attempt was made to find the root cause of the disturbances, which now involved groups of students as opposed to earlier incidents involving only one or two students. After extensive probing, it was discovered that federally funded groups were the culprits. In fact, some of those pushing to gain control of the district's communication system were also involved in this troubling action.

Television was a ready and willing companion of the troublemakers. These groups would plan their action against schools, then inform the news media that there would be trouble at specified locations at given times. The media were always present to report on the fake racial bias.

Superintendent's Advisory Committee

Realizing that no one person had a monopoly on ideas and wisdom, throughout my career I had depended upon bright and caring people to critique and offer suggestions for improving schools. Much of my past success might be attributed to ideas and support of these groups who communicated with the community and offered validity to my approaches.

I had discovered a rich source of brainpower in Jackson as I worked with the group that devised the adopted desegregation plan. So, one day I invited most of those, who were locals, to my office for lunch. The central office cafeteria staff served a nice meal in the boardroom. As the guests ate, I talked about things going on in the school district, both positive and negative, and about programs and activities in planning stages, as well as direction envisioned for the district. I asked for honest and open feedback and suggestions.

The feedback generally was very positive. Although no one could possibly be satisfied with where the district was presently, they felt that much progress was being made. A few suggestions were offered relative to approaches for achieving and even expanding the vision. The meeting was exactly what I had hoped for. Then I asked them to serve as my Advisory Committee and to be prepared to meet with me every six weeks or so for lunch with the same type of format as they had just experienced. I emphasized that the title of the committee was an exact description of what I expected it to be: advisory. I assured them that I was soliciting their honest ideas and advice, but that I reserved the right to accept that which I viewed as being helpful and to reject that which I foresaw as inappropriate at the moment. These were the conditions that would be necessary because I had been empowered by the Board of Education to run the system and would be held accountable for my actions and the results. Nevertheless, I needed their ideas and suggestions. All present seemed to accept the proposal with some offering to host meetings from time to time.

The second meeting of the group went well, but the following one caught me by surprise. One member, Phillip Long, a person whose job involved design and development work, with substantial funding and little oversight, came to the meeting with a complete plan drawn up for the Jackson schools. His plan would dramatically change the direction of programs and plans that had been carefully laid, and had received endorsement of the group only a few weeks earlier. This new proposal also changed the function of the Advisory Committee to one that designed and developed direction for the district. This design also proposed a public relations program that would be run from Phillip's office.

Some discussion evolved with only one or two of the members somewhat aware of the contents of the proposal. Other members remained silent until the author of the plan asked me for my reaction. Treading as lightly as I could, I agreed to study the contents but assured Long that those parts that took control away from the administration would have to be rejected. More pressing needs were then discussed, but participation during the remainder of the meeting was rather subdued. As soon as it seemed appropriate, I adjourned the session.

From that day forward when invitations to meetings of the Committee were announced, Phillip was somehow inadvertently overlooked. The Committee continued to function effectively for the duration of my tenure as Superintendent of Schools in Jackson.

After one such meeting, a member said, "Brandon, I just want to tell you that we were shocked and disappointed when the Board announced that you would be the Superintendent. We didn't think you were tough enough to handle the job, but we were wrong. You have a mild manner that betrays your courage."

Sleep Deprivation Problem

My world was a nightmare. I worked long hours after everyone else had gone home. Then many Saturdays and Sunday afternoons I would go to the office and struggle to dig out from under the deluge of paper that inundated me. When I arrived at home I would be too tired to communicate with the family and too frustrated to sleep. I tried counting sheep, praying unceasingly, urging my mind to be blank, and any other means that came to mind. After tossing and turning for three or four hours, I was so depleted of energy that finally I would fall asleep. The next morning I was almost totally drained and had to kick myself out of bed so I could go face more problems. The predicament was that I was forced to outsmart the intruders in order to protect the school district and hopefully to help it survive.

Finally, I had a long talk with myself. The rest I was getting was totally insufficient for me to function in an acceptable manner. I went to the office each morning too tired to work efficiently and effectively. I controlled my emotions rather well at work, but I was irritable and cross with my family. This had to stop. I convinced myself that lack of sleep and rest would be my downfall unless I took control of my mind and emotions and made some notable changes. "If I'm going to do my job well, I've got to have rest," I reasoned. "Worry helps nothing: it just keeps me awake. If I sleep and relax, I can do a much better job, so from now on, I'm leaving my job at the office. I'm going to sleep, and I'll take up tomorrow where I left off today." And I went to sleep.

Harry Prince, Jack Vest, and maybe Al Russell, had been harassed at home and office constantly. Finally Vest had to have an unlisted phone number to protect his family. In contrast, I was never bothered at home. Of course the Klan was not very active at that time. Those who could not handle integrated schools now had settled their children in private or parochial schools. Perhaps after realizing the suffering of previous superintendents, the people decided to have compassion on this one and at least give me a chance to lead. Or maybe they too were worn out.

Cleaning up Congressional Mess

The President and Congress had provided little more than disappointment for the Board of Education and the Superintendent when they refused to let districts use grants for transportation. However, through maneuvering, shifting funds and playing games, busses and related services were provided as ordered. But the greatest frustration came from the denial of funds for the initial construction of the plazas. The plaza concept was the heart of the desegregation plan and one that the Board couldn't evade. I pondered and poured over the matter for weeks. Not only were funds refused at the federal level, when the State Building Commission was approached about using construction funds accumulated for the Jackson Public Schools, I received strong assurance that state funds would never be approved for building plazas for desegregation purposes.

After studying the various junior high and senior high school facilities and their locations, I met with my Advisory Committee and presented to them the problem I faced. Sam, Jim and the district statistician, Robert Baker, a retired military man, in his late fifties, and a whiz at dealing with numbers related to maps and zones, were present to provide information and to answer questions. After a review of facilities, using an overhead transparency, Dan Owens, a member of the committee said, "You may have to renovate one of the buildings in the north and use it to satisfy the court."

"I'm not nearly as concerned about the court reaction as I am Cohen's," I said. "But if we can come up with the right plan, I believe I can get his approval."

An hour of work and discussion resulted in a prime possibility for a North Plaza facility. Sam felt that the state could not easily deny state construction funds to the district if the application showed that the funds would be used to renovate an existing building. Such denial had never been known. So, I adjourned the meeting feeling that a plan had been devised that met the spirit of the court-ordered agreement.

Cohen's Second Visit

Armed with clarity of thought, overhead transparencies, and refreshments, I received Justin Cohen into my office. This was the second time Cohen had been invited to the Superintendent's office; something to which he was about to become accustomed.

I had coffee and freshly baked cookies brought in. While munching and sipping, I broached the subject by reminding Justin that none of the money for construction that had been promised by federal officials was approved. Then I told him that state construction funds had also been denied. "Hell, I'll sue the state and get the damn money," Cohen threatened.

"I'd rather not do that if we can find a way around it, and I think we can," I assured. "First, there aren't enough state funds available to build even half of one Plaza, and secondly, we need to rebuild our relations with the State Department of Education and the State Superintendent who controls the Building Commission. We'll need them later," I explained.

I reviewed the layout of the district, which was nothing new to Justin who had memorized more details than I would ever know. Looking at the location of schools, I pointed out a fairly new, well-maintained, formerly white, junior high school building in an ideal location for the North Plaza. With an overhead transparency of the current classroom arrangement in place and another depicting the arrangement after renovation, I described how the plaza concept could be achieved without federal funds, provided state funds would be approved for this project. Justin asked if he could borrow the transparencies and said he would need some time to consider the change. Before departing, he asserted that the idea had great possibilities.

I was so certain that Justin would gain approval for the plan from the black community that I began preparing my presentation to the Board of Education. But first, I asked Jim, Sam, Robert Baker, and Gregg Lewis, the school architect, a tall, slim, quiet, blond fellow in his thirties, to prepare an application for state funds, but to place as little emphasis as possible on the Plaza concept. Instead, "Just point out that the building will be renovated to house fifth and sixth grade students, and show as few details in the drawings as possible for satisfying the State Building Commission." The State Superintendent of Education, in effect, was the commission.

Within 48 hours of the discussion with Justin Cohen about the revised plan, I received a call of concurrence from him. I told him that attorney Ulmus would prepare this revision in writing and send it to him for signature, then forward it to the court. This approved revision paved the way for the staff to begin clearing hurdles for developing the first Plaza.

Plaza Revision Presented to Board

The new approach to satisfying the court was presented to the Board of Education for approval. Few details were presented publicly except for the fact that this junior high school building would be renovated and house fifth and sixth grade students the coming school year. A second item presented for approval was permission to apply for construction funds accumulated by the state for the Jackson schools. Both items were passed unanimously without discussion. The third item was the creation a position of Assistant Superintendent of Fifth/Sixth Grade Centers. This recommendation was approved also.

The innovative education complex, to be successful, would require much more than accommodating facilities. The program would be the most important item in gaining parental acceptance. Moving from self-contained classrooms into large open space areas, with teachers working as teams, would require significant training. Then, appropriate materials for meeting a great range of abilities and achievement levels would be required. A large part of the materials would have to be designed, developed and printed. Material storage and access to them had to be considered carefully. The planning required for this monster to be successful would be monumental.

With plans moving smoothly toward the development of the North Plaza, the South Plaza was placed on hold. No funds were available for constructing the second complex and none could be projected in the foreseeable future. However, the perceived dilemma was not made public because the efforts of the Board in implementing the court directed North Plaza were sufficient to assure good faith for the time being.

Chapter 10

Events and Incidents of Note

Anonymous Letter Writer Discovered

Saturday morning, as usual, found me in the office trying to catch up on important mail, do reflective thinking and planning, and do a little professional reading. I often spent Sunday afternoons or evenings the same way. On this particular morning as I was going through the stacks of paper on my desk, I ran across a small typewritten note from Jim Minor. A thought hit my mind. "Jim Minor has a typewriter on his desk with which he does his own personal typing. Is it possible that the anonymous letter that brought me here was written by Jim?" Hurriedly, I flipped through some files in my desk drawer and immediately found the letter I had received at my office at Auburn University. Being alone in the central office, I made my way into Jim's office, a well-known forbidden area, in his absence.

I stepped back into the hallway, made my way to the copy machine and retrieved a clean sheet of copy paper. Back in Jim's office I inserted it in the typewriter and began replicating the anonymous letter. Upon completion, I climbed into my car and headed for the local police crime laboratory where I deposited both drafts of the letter for examination.

A short time later, I received a report which read, in part:

> The letters in this case consist of a type written anonymous letter . . . .
> The other letter is a sample of type from a typewriter in the office building
> of the questioned and known. There is a slight misalignment in the small
> letter "t" in both the known and questioned. The type face is making a

deeper impression on the right side than the left. The small letter "i" in both . . . bear perhaps a class characteristic in that the vertical bar does not intersect the lower serif at the midpoint, but off to the left side.

The type on both the known and questioned is of the elite type. There is a defect in the small letter "e" in both the questioned and known. This can be seen in the curved portion of the vertical loop which is slightly flattened out. There is an absence of a serif in the middle stroke of the letter "m" in both . . . .

Not really surprised, I began contemplating what I should do with the report. The situation seldom left my mind during the next two days. Finally, I decided to take the anonymous letter and the crime lab report to Bob Ross and discuss the matter with him. On Wednesday, my secretary arranged an appointment with the Board Chairman for 10:00 a.m. the following day.

I arrived on time for the appointment and was greeted by Ross, escorted into his office where I reached back and closed the door. I told Mr. Ross the reason I had come to Jackson, and showed him the anonymous letter. I explained how I had replicated the letter. Then I showed Mr. Ross the lab report. Bob Ross turned exceedingly red-faced and was perhaps the angriest man I had ever seen. "Fire that Son-of-a-Bitch and he will be the firedest Son-of-a-Bitch in the world," Ross screamed.

Calmly, I said, "I don't want to fire him. I just want you to know about this and you can inform the other board members if you like. He's a valuable man in many respects and I'd like to keep him, but if he ever creates another problem or tries to defy me, I'll recommend his dismissal."

Mr. Ross, still shaken, said, "I depended on Jim Minor more than any staff member, other than the superintendent, to provide me accurate information. If I'd not seen the evidence I'd never have believed he'd done such a thing. I've received probably 50 anonymous letters since I've been on the Board and I never suspected they came from him. But now that I have read that letter, I can hear ole Minor's voice in every one of them. I think you should fire the Son-of-a-Bitch."

"Let's just wait awhile and see how he works out. If I need to, I'll be back," I assured him.

Jim was a prolific note writer. Sometimes they were typed on sheets from small note pads, or maybe on an entire page in longhand, but more often they were notes in the margins of memos with which he disagreed. Interoffice notes usually carried his initials or signature, while supposedly anonymous notes were typed and mailed to my home address. He was great at passing along information in his anonymous notes relative to transgressions. One such note, a follow-up to a previous note, was as follows:

> *I wrote you earlier about a romance that exists in the Central Office. Mrs. Wills and Mr. Windslow both left work Tuesday and met in Parshner Park down Highway 55 South. They were gone three hours of school time.*

I called Mr. Windslow to my office to discuss the matter. When Windslow denied the allegation, he was given a stern warning and sent back to his job.

One evening when I arrived home, Wanda handed me a letter addressed to me. Upon opening it I found inside a copy of a letter-to-the-editor from some newspaper. The writer said that a person with an earned doctor's degree was usually much less capable than one who had an honorary doctorate. The reason for this differential is that honorary degrees are bestowed upon people who have proven to be outstanding in their area of work whereas the earned degree only assures academic ability, not the ability to perform in a superior manner.

After reading the article, I threw it in the kitchen waste can. I knew that Dr. Harry Prince had an honorary degree and that the writer, or at least the one who mailed it, had to be a Prince admirer and that was fine with me because I too admired Dr. Prince for his intellectual and administrative abilities and for his personal character.

That evening in bed, before going to sleep, I asked Wanda to retrieve the article from the trash can when she went to the kitchen to prepare breakfast.

Surprised, she asked, "why."

"I'm going to mail it to Mr. Minor tomorrow," I responded.

"What in the world will he think when he gets it?" she asked.

"If he didn't mail it to me he won't know what to think, but if he did, he will know that I am on to his anonymous letter writing scheme." Sure enough, that was the last anonymous letter I received, with one exception. Furthermore, Jim Minor was a different person after that when around me.

Another Type of Anonymous Letter

A letter arrived in my Office that contained a short note and ten dollars. The note said something to the effect that, *"When I attended school in Jackson I stole a pencil and crayon one day. My conscience has bothered me these many years and I am sending $10 to cover the cost of the items. I am extremely sorry for what I did."*

There was no signature and the postmark on the envelope showed that it was mailed from another state.

Women Meet With School Chief

Two female teachers, Emma Patterson, a tall, well built, high school teacher, neatly dressed in black and white plaid skirt and white blouse, approximately 50, excellent in speech and poise; and Kelley Grace, a young, attractive, petite, elementary teacher wearing a mini-skirt appeared in my office, as scheduled. They were there to discuss what they considered to be a major concern of teachers. This was the era of the mini-skirt. Teachers were concerned that they were prohibited by the district dress code from wearing pants. The current style was somewhat difficult to manage, particularly in elementary grades where teachers had to move around the room helping students and correcting work. This part of the job required them to bend over.

Several teachers had discussed the problem, and asked these two teachers to meet with me and request that the teacher dress code be revised to permit the wearing of pantsuits. They both assured me that they wanted to dress nicely and would not deviate from the requested code.

Having visited a preschool class in Harlem a few years earlier, I was inclined to agree with the teachers. The mini-skirt probably had its origin in the Big Apple, and the teacher of this class not only wore a mini-skirt but a very loose, low-cut blouse. No matter which way she turned, she was constantly exposing herself. The teachers of Jackson were good people who wanted to please. There were few troublemakers. These women were sincere in their request and it was granted immediately.

Parental Concerns about Integrated Schools

My experience during the call-in radio show was indicative of concerns that many white parents had about desegregation. A middle school teacher related to me a conversation she had with a mother of one of her students. The mother said, "I can't believe the words my son is learning at school. He comes home and I find that he uses the most vulgar words known. I just don't know if we can keep him in public schools."

The teacher asked, "Has he used any words that were new to you or that have meanings that you didn't understand?"

"Well, no, not really," she replied hesitatingly.

"Then these words must have been used in segregated schools when you were younger?" she inquired.

"I guess they were," the mother admitted.

A major concern of many white parents was that their children might become romantically involved with black students. Chances are good that black parents had similar concerns but I was not told this. These worries were not totally without foundation. A white co-ed at one high school, the daughter of a middle class Jackson family, academically bright, and overweight, began slipping away in the evenings seeing a black male student. Soon she was pregnant and eventually told her parents about her condition. They could not accept the situation. They became very angry and refused to let the girl come home. Parents of the black boy would not let her come to their home either. Soon the girl somehow arranged for a backroom abortion. Still her parents would not accept her and, because neighbors knew of the situation, the family moved away. The girl disappeared.

Another situation of a similar nature turned out much better. The girl involved was a beautiful and talented high school cheerleader, and the only child of a rather well-known couple. She began dating a black boy, on the sly, but eventually told her parents that they were madly in love and wanted to get married. The family tried to get her to end the relationship but she finally told them she was pregnant. They were greatly disappointed, but with much reluctance accepted the fact and supported her. The ceremony was performed in private, and several months later a beautiful baby girl was born. The child became a vital part of this active family, but after two years the mixed couple divorced.

Perhaps an even greater concern of white parents was that the academic quality of schools would diminish. There was considerable basis for this worry, not because it had to be that way, but because the sudden change in Jackson, brought about by dogged resistance to desegregation, provided no time for administrators and teachers to prepare and be retrained to deal with the drastically changed classroom condition. Black students had received an inferior education and, generally, were far behind white students in academic achievement. Teachers had been trained and experienced in teaching students who were more nearly alike in background and achievement and had been given a standard procedure and timeline for teaching. Suddenly, the students were so diverse that teacher backgrounds were a greater hindrance than help. Difficult is the task of undoing deeply imbedded learning and in absorbing new ways of teaching. The assumption usually is that "this new-fangled approach" would have been used historically had it been effective, so we are not about to change.

Problems Continue To Pop Up

Just when I began to think things were running smoothly, a new problem would occur. One Saturday morning while in my office the phone rang. Upon answering, I heard an apologetic voice saying, "This is James Hale. I hate to call you but I have a major problem and need help. My daughter, Jean, is a first year teacher at Brooks Elementary School. She was working in her room Friday afternoon preparing for Monday and didn't realize that all other teachers were gone for the day. When she went to the office to sign out, the principal became too familiar with her and when she resisted, he caught her by the arm and tried to force her into his office. Resisting strongly, she broke away and quickly left the building. She doesn't want to resign but neither does she want to return to the school." I assured the man that I would take care of the problem immediately. I told him that his daughter should return to work on Monday, and for her own success on the job, she should not say one word about the incident to anyone.

As soon as I hung up the phone, I call two assistants, Johnny Wise and Lawson McCreary and asked them to be in my office at 2:00 p.m. the following day. Then I called the Principal, Mike Goode, and asked him to be present at the same time.

Sunday afternoon when everyone was present, I presented the information I had received then asked what he would have done if the teacher had gone into the office with him. The Principal said, "I would have been a man."

I asked if there were any questions, and when no one responded, I said to the Principal, "You are not to report to work again. You can resign or I will recommend your dismissal to the Board. You can let me know tomorrow which you prefer."

Monday morning, I called Justin Cohen and explained the situation. Justin said," Let me handle this." Later Monday, Mr. Goode and his wife, Sue, came to my office and asked that the decision to dismiss him be withdrawn because he did nothing to the girl. I refused their request. Before the week was over, principal Goode had resigned.

Gnawing Racial Incidents

Having grown up and worked in schools where there were few disturbances, I was always amazed when acts of violence or vandalism occurred, or when racial hatred reared its head. The number of incidents in Jackson's schools was small and minor in comparison to those which were occurring in larger cities, particularly in the Mid-west and Northeast. Yet they were unacceptable and troubling to me.

Near the end of the school year, prior to assuming the superintendency, there were a number of student walkouts and an occasional fight involving both boys and girls. If the fight was between students of the same race, they were seldom reported; however, if it was between those of different races it got quick attention and almost always made the news, both TV and newspaper. One or more times, tensions between the races resulted in school closings.

The first such episode occurring during my tenure resulted from a white boy throwing an object onto the food tray of a black girl. Fights between groups of four or five students of each race erupted that afternoon after school. This was the first such incident at that particular high school where race relations had been excellent. But there were a few of each race who were always ready to either create or take up any racial cause.

About a month later, crudely executed sheets containing some school administrators' names and telephone numbers were sent to about 10 white female teachers. The circular offered white teachers $500 for maneuvering a black male into a compromising position and arranging for a friend to witness the affair which could result in the expulsion of black male students or dismissal of black male teachers. Of course the whole thing was absurd but it caused a flap in the black community and required some PR work.

Human Relations Team Formed

Significant strides in racial acceptance were being made in some schools, while in others, little or no progress was observable. The occasional flare-ups and unceasing racial tension in isolated areas made it imperative that the district move offensively to overcome these difficulties. After considerable staff discussion, a decision was made to establish a Human Relations Team consisting of two people, one black and one white. Both had to be highly respected for the work they had done in their own schools in establishing and maintaining calm and an orderly environment. Grant funds were available for just such an activity.

Two principals were selected and enticed to accept the assignment under the condition that it was temporary, and that acting principals of their choosing would be assigned. They hated to leave their schools but saw the urgency for such assistance with both staff and students. The Team would work with both students and staff. They would meet monthly with a student committee in each high school; however, most of their work would be on an as-needed basis. These two would have great latitude in establishing their own schedules.

The First Threat

One Saturday evening Wanda and I slipped away to a restaurant in an adjoining community to enjoy some privacy and a good meal. While waiting for the food to arrive, Wanda asked, "Who is that man over there that keeps looking at us?"

At an appropriate time I looked at the table Wanda had pointed out. "I have no idea," I replied.

"Well he can't seem to keep his eyes off us," she said.

"Maybe he's just admiring you the way I always have," I jokingly responded.

"I don't like him staring at us," she said conclusively.

The food was served, and we enjoyed the meal, as much as one could enjoy eating while under constant surveillance. As soon as we had finished, I called for the check, paid the bill, and we left the restaurant. The door had scarcely closed when the man who had been watching us rushed up to me and abruptly said, "Just a minute. I have some things to say to you."

I wheeled around facing the man and said, "Let's hear it."

"I want you to know that we are sick and tired of them damn niggers jumping our boys at school. You better get the sons-of-bitches straightened out or we will."

"And who are we?" I asked.

"The Klan. You may think that we have disbanded but we are watching your every move," he responded.

Stepping forward until bodies and noses almost touched and with every ounce of authority my voice could muster, I replied, "You are the troublemakers. You're the ones who encourage white boys to badger the blacks, both boys and girls. Well I'm sick and tired of you and your kind, and I deeply regret that you and I are even of the same race because I'm ashamed of you and your bigotry. You are not even worthy of being called a human. You and your kind are nothing but sneaking rats, undeserving to live. Buddy, let me tell you something. You had better call off the dogs. I'm not afraid of you or the Klan, in the least, but you'd better be afraid because you will change or be hunted down and destroyed. Do you have anything else to say?"

At that, the man turned and went back inside the restaurant, and Wanda and I got in our car and headed toward Jackson.

"I'm scared to death," Wanda said as she shook.

"Afraid of what?" I asked calmly.

"The Klan," she replied."

"They're nothing but a bunch of cowards when confronted," I assured her.

"We'll have a cross burned in our yard tonight. You can count on that," Wanda insisted.

"So what? They are nothing but cowards. If they want to burn a cross, let them, but they will never scare me, and you shouldn't be afraid either. In my opinion, it's all over, but they sure ruined a rare evening for us."

Bus Drivers Threaten Strike

No large school district in America had experienced peace in the last 10 years, so why should Jackson be any different? Unrest among unionized city bus drivers soon spread to the school district drivers as organizers attempted to pull these drivers into the Transit Union.

Just prior to schools closing for Christmas holidays, a list of demands was placed before the administration with rumors galore about a strike deadline. The Bus Supervisor determined that some mistakes of earlier years had been carried over to the present, and indeed, wage changes were overdue, and adult drivers should be placed on the state plan of retirement with the district paying a percentage of the contribution to the retirement system. While many were steeped in the holiday spirit and singing Christmas carols, the administration and Board were designing a plan to bring harmony to a rightly disgruntled group of employees. The first public school announcement of 1972 was the agreement between the Board of Education and its bus drivers.

Transfer Teachers or Lose Funds

A threatened bus strike had hardly been avoided when another calamity occurred. HEW presented a report from its monitoring of the Jackson schools and noted that the district had failed to maintain the 60/40 ratio of white to black teachers as prescribed by court order. The notice demanded that 23 teachers be transferred immediately to restore the ratio.

I appealed to the Atlanta office of HEW to allow the district to delay the transfer to the end of the school year since I was new in office and was unaware of the deviation. As usual with those bureaucrats, it was now or lose funding. So, 23 teachers were transferred. I promised to get them back to their schools at the beginning of the next school year, but one resigned rather than move. Others reluctantly accepted their new assignments; however, this additional example of instability probably caused a number of white students to withdraw from public education.

It seemed that the courts, HEW and civil rights activists could never get the point that they were driving whites from public schools so rapidly that instead of having integrated schools they were on the threshold of segregation again, a point that over several years was realized.

New Secondary Plan Approved By Court

In late January, a new desegregation plan for junior and senior high schools was announced. The new order, recommended by all parties and approved by the court, was a distinct improvement over the previous plan. As trust between the races improved, both could be more objective in designing a plan. The plaintiff had viewed with disbelief the massive withdrawal of white students who were zoned into formerly all-black schools in ghetto-type areas and the tremendous damage done by establishing one-and two-grade schools.

An announcement by the Superintendent of the new plan said, in part:

> . . . . *We have been working on modifications that would eliminate these one-and two-grade centers and take us back to the three-grade junior high school and three-grade senior high school. With this plan, students will attend only two schools during their last six years of schooling. While no plan will be satisfactory to everyone, we do believe that the modifications we are proposing will be very pleasing to the vast majority, will lend stability to the program, and will permit us to develop a sequence in each school to better meet the needs of boys and girls . . . . These changes indicate the progress that is being made in educational improvements and in the development of trust between the black and white communities. With continued community support, we can have the kind of educational programs we all desire . . . .*

Still there were problems that desperately needed to be solved. An example was the court's order to transfer Reserve Officers Training Corp (ROTC) and the vocational shops to a school that was in an area of the city where few white adults dared to go. The mistaken idea was that these programs would serve as a magnet to attract white students who were already in the programs, as well as younger students who would like the specialized training. If the judges had, on their own, without guide or guard, gone to the school, they would have known that white students would not attend. But the plaintiff pushed the idea, and the court could not be persuaded to reject it. Efforts to correct this problem were rejected by plaintiff with the stipulation that it could be discussed later.

Walter Cronkite Interview

Much progress was being made in the Jackson schools, and articles of a positive nature began to appear in newspapers and magazines in different parts of the country. A call from the Walter Cronkite Show was received by the district Public Relations office asking to interview the Superintendent the following day at 10:00 a.m.

Upon arrival, the TV crew, escorted by the PR director, Art Seaborne, scouted the central office area and decided that the best location was in front of the building with the Jackson Municipal Separate School District sign in the background. When the equipment was in place and made ready, Hilda Langford came to my office to notify me that they were ready to talk. This was a very cold day, and I went outside with my hands in my pockets, followed by Hilda. She hurried up beside me and quietly said, "Keep your hands out of your pockets. The seat of your pants is split from top to bottom." After that, the interview proceeded, but I was not quite sure how it went. Some of the staff who observed the interview assured me that it went well.

Search for Community Support

Prompted by some of the more liberal and tolerant leaders of the community, the Board requested that a Jackson Education Task Force be established to interpret and communicate the desegregation plan to the community, to disseminate information on school assignments, and generally, to couch court orders in positive terms, thus deflecting some of the anticipated resentment away from the Board. The Task Force, diverse in composition, drew people from well-respected organizations.

Additionally, several members of the Task Force, and others encouraged by the group, volunteered to serve as speakers at civic clubs, churches, PTA meetings or any gatherings that ask for speakers. In a number of instances, meetings were held in homes with neighbors invited to hear the speakers and to ask questions about the school situation.

I spent much effort in actively using the District PTA Council to revitalize the PTA in each and every school, and encouraging it to become a strong support base for the school district. Solid leadership emerged giving impetus to the public relations efforts to save the schools. Although no one knew what the new school year would bring, the Task Force and the PTA were delivering a strong, reassuring message to the community.

Church Address by Superintendent

I responded positively to the many invitations to meet with and speak to various small groups. Churches were quick to ask me to meet either with groups from their congregations or to fill the pulpit, thereby engaging the entire congregation. I considered these invitations as opportunities to inform and educate the community on what was happening as well as what could happen in the schools. With many institutions of higher education in Jackson, I knew that I would reach a large number of professors in my church presentations. They needed to know where we were headed with the schools because they could be a great ally or a dangerous enemy. My presentations in major churches were tailored for a well-educated, sophisticated clientele, whereas other presentations were designed for that particular audience. Each talk gave me an opportunity to reassure the public and to solicit support for the schools. Following is a large part of the text of one such presentation in one of Jackson's major downtown churches:

> *During the past several days my secretary, almost daily, asked me, in a joking way, when I was going to prepare my sermon. Perhaps it is because of my sinful ways, but her use of the word "sermon" tended to make me a bit uncomfortable.*
>
> *Most Jacksonians will tell you that this city has had fine schools for many years. Jackson does have a history of providing quality academic instruction for students both at the elementary and secondary level as well as the college level. I was having lunch with an elderly gentleman last week when the subject of education came up and he remarked that "We had one of the finest school systems in the nation before the mess." From my observation, I would say that Jackson had a superior college preparatory program for a long period of time. There was little emphasis on vocational education or the teaching of saleable skills. For the past several years there has been a growing emphasis on education for the handicapped even though at this time there is not a program for all handicapped children.*
>
> *And then desegregation came. In some places desegregation was a gradual process. In Jackson it happened all at once. Generally I would*

say that a sudden impact is bad; however, who knows what would have happened had the process been gradual here. The thing I know and you know is that desegregation caused a terrible shock, and to some extent it caused uncertainty, confusion and turmoil. But I want to reassure you by promising that out of this turmoil will emanate the best education for all students that Jackson has ever known, because now the focus is on improvement, not on maintaining the status quo. Education will no longer cater to one group; instead it will be concerned with all.

Education, of necessity, must be concerned with societal goals. Only a few years ago there was a tremendous shortage of college-trained people, and the hue and cry was for more people to go to college. Educators urged all who were capable to attend college. Our nation has become more and more an affluent society, colleges have become overcrowded, and our college graduates have become too numerous. As a result, lots of engineers are driving trucks, and many trained teachers are working in dime stores. Now the cry is for more and more technically trained individuals. Right now, the city of Jackson needs more people available with technical skills in order to compete for new industries. I am told that during the 1980's only 17 per cent of the jobs available will require a college degree. Only eight per cent will require individuals with no technical training. In other words, during the 1980's it appears that 75 per cent of the work force of this nation will have had some kind of technical training to prepare them for their job.

What then should be the goals of our schools? I would suggest that this school district needs a comprehensive program; a program that will help all individuals to achieve their goals. We must continue to be vitally concerned with the academic preparation for those pupils who will pursue a college degree. We must be equally concerned with those who would pursue vocational or technical skills after high school graduation, and with those who desire to learn a saleable skill during their high school years. Presently a very high percentage of our high school graduates go to college. But an unheralded statistic is that nearly half of our students drop out of school prior to graduation. We must develop programs that meet the needs of the individuals so they stay in school and pursue worthwhile goals.

Our program is rapidly expanding to the point of serving all handicapped children. We have not reached the point of providing service for all who need it, but we are rapidly approaching the time when we will be able to do this. We have an opportunity now to push forward in the field of handicapped services, but the time is at hand when we will be forced to provide these services if we don't do it voluntarily.

A comprehensive program of public education should not stop with those enrolled in grades 1 through 12, but should extend literally from the cradle to the grave. The Jackson Public School system employed a firm to conduct a needs assessment study in this city. The report indicated that the people of this community feel that the two greatest needs in Jackson area are an outstanding vocational education program and a preschool program. The State Department of Education also conducted a needs assessment study for the state of Mississippi. The number one need, according to the people of this state is a preschool program. Those who know much about child development and the learning process are quick to say that we would be better off educationally to do away with the twelfth grade and add a kindergarten program to our education system. We are retarding the intellectual growth of many of our children through failure to develop a formal preschool program. Many of you are aware that the Jackson School District has initiated a daycare program for a rather small group of preschool children. This is being done through the use of federal funds. But I am looking forward to the day when preschool training will be available to all of the children of Jackson.

And finally, a comprehensive educational program must not neglect the adults of the community. I am sure that many of you are unaware of the extensive adult education program presently available in the Jackson School System. We now serve from three to five thousand adults annually through our adult education program. A continuous program is offered adults whereby they can obtain a high school diploma. In addition to that, we offer courses in almost any subject when twelve or more adults wish to enroll and when a teacher can be found to teach the course. But our adult education program needs to go far beyond its present state.

The time will come, and I hope it will be very soon, when we will be permitted to build a vocational facility or facilities which will serve all of the high schools of Jackson. Schools are always limited in the amount of funds available to provide the services which are desired; however, I hope that when such facilities are available, we will be able to combine our funds with funds from other sources to keep the vocational school operating, conceivably, 24 hours a day. I know of no reason why students who pursue an academic program during the regular school day could not learn a technical skill or trade during the evening. I know of no reason, provided funds are available, why the same facilities could not be used to train those adults who do not have technical skills, and who are unable to find gainful employment because of lack of skills. Neither do I know of reasons why adults who are gainfully employed should not be permitted to sharpen the skills which they already have, or to learn entirely different skills which would enable them to move to higher paying positions. In other words, it seems to me that a vocation facility should serve many people, both school age and older, in the community.

During the past few years it has been almost impossible to do any advance planning, particularly as related to building needs. As a result of little or no long range planning for buildings, this school district now has in use approximately 175 portable classrooms. This is the equivalent of four or five high schools or eight or nine elementary schools. The building boom which Jackson is experiencing, the planned development of large areas of the city, and the proposed expansion of city boundaries make it imperative that we examine our building needs and plan a program and schedule for meeting these needs.

The staff of the Jackson School District began two years ago to precisely define academic skills that children are expected to learn. Great progress has been made in carrying out this project and in putting the results to use. Through the definition of skills it becomes possible to be rather accurate in placement of pupils, in prescribing educational treatment, and in evaluating behavioral changes brought about through this process of learning. Philosophers might tell you that a conflict exists between the behaviorist who believes in defining skills, in placement, prescription and evaluation, and the humanist who believes that the behavioral approach is inhumane. The reason for this apparent conflict is that each defines his philosophy in its purest form and points out the contradictions inherent in the two philosophies. It is my strong belief that there is not inherent conflict in the two approaches, but it is only through a marriage of the two that learning become most efficient and effective and that humaneness is actually a necessary component of a behaviorally oriented program which functions properly.

I was asked to speak on the future of public education in Jackson, but I was not told how far into the future I was to look. I mentioned the behaviorist and humanistic approaches in order to offer assurance that come what may, I think we are on the right track. Now I don't know exactly what is going to happen in the future as far as education is concerned, but I can tell you this much—education is going to be different from what it has been in the past. I think it is sure to become more electronically oriented, and the chances are good that the focus is going back to public education because expense involved in moving into the electronic age in education is likely to be too expensive for most privately supported schools. The refinement and further development of computers is going to have a terrific impact upon education. The computer, tied in with electronic retrieval systems, broadcast capabilities and the development of cassette video could well change the whole system of educating children, particularly those at the secondary and college levels.

It appears to me that it is economically feasible for many services provided through federal, state and local municipalities to be consolidated so that recreation, education, public libraries, etc., could be located on one site utilizing the latest equipment and techniques. The facilities could serve many purposes. The school itself could become an education center where pupils would come for their assignments, then return to their home, their library, or to some other place where, through the use of electronic equipment mentioned earlier, tied into the telephone system, would be able to have at their command the information to help them to complete their assignment or to reach a point where it would be necessary for them to return to the education center for individual consultation, or for seminars, or for other activities vital to their program of study.

I could go on and on talking with you about possible trends in education, but they would be mere speculations. Again, I predict that education will be different in the future than it is today. I will also predict that it will be more efficient because tax revolts lead to efficiency, and I believe that we are all rather certain that people are getting tired of having their taxes raised. That is one of the reasons why I believe that in the future, the City of Jackson and its public school system will work hand in hand in acquiring property, building facilities, and financing programs that serve large segment of the community through multiple uses of facilities.

Great progress has been made in the last year or two in bringing about educational change and in improving the educational programs of the Jackson Public Schools. I am very proud of Jacksonians, and I am especially proud of the vast majority of the leaders of this community because of the encouragement and support they have given to the public schools. I am aware of the fears, frustrations and uncertainty that have been present during the past few years, but let me say to you that the changes which have occurred have brought an unremitting commitment and devotion to improving education for all the people.

I have never been more optimistic about the possibilities for educational greatness than I am today. There have been headlines in national publications which were unbecoming to Mississippi and to the City of Jackson. But more recently there have been more favorable headlines in reference to Jackson's public schools. We have the opportunity to provide leadership for this nation in the development, refinement and implementation of an outstanding educational program. Let me assure you that with your continued encouragement and support we will develop a system of public schools that will be second to none in this nation.

Lesson in Boardsmanship

A member of the Jackson Board decided he didn't want to be reappointed by the City Council, so he was replaced with Rayburn Olsen, an up-and-coming young professional, trim, outgoing, in his 30's. Bob Ross administered the oath of office to the new member, welcomed him aboard, and told him that the Board had always worked together well, and he would be expected to fit into the tradition.

The Superintendent's office was the gathering place for Board Members prior to each meeting, and when all were present, they would walk together to the boardroom and proceed with official business. Business was never discussed prior to going to the boardroom. This was a chance for members and the Superintendent to do a little socializing and catching up on news. In the first pre-meeting gathering attended by Olsen, he said, "If anyone wants to hear my maiden speech as a Board Member, you should attend the Civitan meeting Tuesday."

Mr. Ross's ears perked up, and he asked, "You mean you are speaking as a Board Member?"

"Yes Sir," the new member responded.

"And just what are you going to tell this group?" Ross asked.

"I'm going to tell them what should be done to improve our schools," he explained.

Bob Ross vaulted to his feet, stuck his finger in Olsen's face, and angrily responded, "The only time you are a board member is when we are in an official meeting. Other than at that time you don't have an opinion. You don't know a thing about running the schools. We have a Superintendent and staff to do that. If you want to make speeches, come to the Superintendent and ask him what to say, and stick to that script.

We will **not** have six different voices speaking to this community. Let me assure you of one thing right now. If you ever promise anything, this Board will see that it is never delivered."

Mr. Ross sat down amid a completely hushed audience. I could not remember another word being said until I said, "We'd better get to the boardroom."

Kickback or What?

Beth Noles said, "Dr. Sparkman, Henry Long wants to talk with you on the phone."

Mr. Long said, "Dr. Sparkman, you remember the re-plumbing job we approved recently?"

"You mean the one at Westside High School," I inquired, as if there had been another re-plumbing job approved.

"Yeah! Well I just had a call from one of the bidders who told me that he had checked the proposed job carefully and that it was totally unneeded. He says the fresh water lines are copper and will never need replacing. And the water lines from the boiler to the radiators look perfectly good. He smells a rat."

"Thanks Mr. Long," I responded. "I'll look into it immediately."

I called Jim Minor to my office and questioned him about the re-plumbing job that he had recommended.

Jim said, "I took Ray Smith's (plumbing foreman) word that it was needed. I certainly don't have the time or knowledge to inspect after every recommendation. I have to depend on my men, and in this case, I don't think I have been misled."

I placed a long distance phone call to a friend in my home state that was a well-respected heating and plumbing engineer. I relayed the information I had about the job that was being bid, and asked if he could come to Jackson on the weekend and assess the situation. He agreed.

Next, I called Lawson McCreary to my office and explained the problem. I asked him to meet with me and the engineer on Saturday afternoon and accompany the engineer to the building. He should be certain that the engineer had access to all areas of the building, including the ability to crawl through any spaces underneath the building. Furthermore, this situation and the inspection were to be discussed with no one. When the inspection was completed, he and the engineer were to return to my office. Lawson agreed to the assignment.

On Saturday afternoon with the inspection completed, the three of us met in my office. The assessment was that the fresh water pipes that were scheduled for replacement were in great condition. The hot water lines from the boiler and the return lines showed no external defects. The engineer suggested that the lines perhaps needed to be graded to assure proper flow, but other than that he saw nothing that needed to be done. He recommended that a three-foot piece of the line that the plumbing foreman considered to be in worst condition be cut out and sent to him for analysis.

On Monday, I called Ray Smith to my office and questioned him about the need for the re-plumbing job. Smith stated that he was constantly called to the school because of leaks in the water lines from the boiler. Pipes were patched and sections replaced regularly because they were paper thin from rust and long use he contended. Since no heat was needed at that time of year, I asked him to accompany Lawson McCreary to the school, search and find the worst segment of pipe, and cut a three foot section out and bring it to my office. This he did.

I could see no noticeable thinness or severe rusting, but I shipped the pipe to the engineer. Within the week a phone call came that the pipe was in good condition except for minor buildup inside that could be corrected by use of a chemical in the boiler.

I proceeded to meet with the architect who had prepared the plans and specifications for the replacement. While appearing highly nervous, his only statement was, "I did what I was told to do." He refused to answer any questions.

Ray Smith was dismissed, and the Board stopped the bidding process without any public explanation for doing so. I was certain other bidders knew the reason. I asked Henry Long to call the prospective bidder who blew the whistle and thank him for his service.

An Outsider's View of Jackson

In the spring of 1972, I was invited to be Guest Lecturer at Florida Atlantic University where I spoke on the subject of "Desegregation: Impetus for Curriculum and Social Change." The stage was set by describing Jackson's school situation "then" and "now." As I completed my address, I suggested that my listeners could get a more objective picture of Jackson by reading an article by John Egerton entitled, *"Report Card on Southern School Desegregation"* in the April 1, 1972 issue of *Saturday Review.*

The article compares and contrasts the Jackson schools and the Nashville, Tennessee schools relative to their handling of desegregation. It depicts the problems and progress in Jackson as a turnaround in attitude and action. Egerton describes the "hapless record of no wins and eleven defeats in its court fight against integration . . . ." He then says, "It is little short of astonishing, then, that when a new plan using busing to desegregate . . . was put into effect last fall it had official and explicit encouragement from the Jackson Chamber of Commerce." But, he pointed to the decline in enrollment of about 9000 white pupil within the next few months.

"Jackson's schools appear to be in a state of balance between the past and future, between segregation and integration." Egerton pointed out that the future depends upon a lot of ifs: "if a start is made on the educational parks, if black teachers and principals gain a sense of confidence that their jobs are secure, if new teachers and administrators hired by the system raise the over-all levels of quality and sensitivity, if an upcoming school board appointment continues the trend toward biracial strength in that important body, and if white flight to private schools has peaked out and begins to reverse, then Mississippi's largest city may be on its way to quality and equality . . ."

"Superintendent Sparkman, who appears to have a broad base of support from both black and white segments of the community, maintains a soft-spoken optimism about the future," he concludes[3]

Meeting with Governor

This was the era of numerous federal program grants, some of which required the recommendation or endorsement of the Governor in order to obtain official grant approval. One such program had significant funds available for the Jackson schools, provided the Governor would recommend the award. Of course, this was the same Governor, John Bell

[3]   Egerton, John, "Report Card of Southern School Desegregation," *Saturday Review*, (April 1, 1972), pp. 41-48.

Williams, who had ordered the cutoff of state funds to the Jackson School District, so there was little hope that he would offer a favorable response.

I knew that Henry Mabry and Shelton Johns, both bankers and members of my advisory committee, were fairly close to the Governor. I discussed the grant situation with the two who decided that a visit with the Governor wouldn't hurt anything and could possibly result in receiving the grant. Henry made an appointment with Governor Williams for 4:00 p.m. on Thursday. The three of us met on the prearranged day and walked to the capitol where we were greeted by the receptionist and escorted into the Governor's office.

The Governor seated us somewhat toward the end of his desk and rotated his chair so that he was virtually facing us. There was a little chit chat before the Governor took control of the conversation with little opportunity afforded for interaction. Shelton interrupted him long enough to advance the purpose of the visit. This intrusion into his story telling was ignored, and Governor Williams continued. Finally, he began a tirade on racial integration and the inferiority of blacks. He said that he had visited the governor of Idaho, and while there, "offered to ship him a train load of Niggers in exchange for a train load of syrup, to which the Idaho Governor said, 'You just keep your Niggers and I'll keep my syrup'."

At this point, I had listened to just about all I could take, so I butted in and said, "Governor, everyone has a right to his own attitude, but yours is the rottenest one I have ever encountered."

"Suddenly, Henry jumped to his feet and said, "I have someone waiting in my office to see me and I must go."

Shelton said, "Yeah, I'm running late for a staff meeting. I have to go also."

So, the Governor and I were alone. I took the initiative to remind Governor Williams of the purpose of the visit. As previously anticipated, the request for endorsement of the grant application was denied.

Wrong Choice Made Right

I talked with Chairman, Bob Ross about approaching Governor William Waller, who had recently been sworn into office, about assisting the Jackson Board in its effort to secure certain state and federal funding. Ross, cleared his throat and said, "Doctor, I was on the wrong side in this election." Then after hesitating briefly, he continued. "But, the Governor's office has new, solid walnut, paneling so I guess I could persuade him to give me an appointment." Mr. Ross got the appointment and a favorable response. At last, Mississippi had a governor who appeared to hold no grudges against the Jackson School District and its administration.

Chapter 11

Organizational Change

I gained a new prospective on running a troubled school district after becoming Superintendent. A friend of mine, while serving as Superintendent of a district similar in size to the Jackson district, once remarked that having served several years as Deputy Superintendent of a much larger troubled district, he felt that he knew just about all there was to know about running a school system. However, upon taking the top job, he realized that he had actually learned little about being in the position where the buck stops.

I was cognizant of some of the problems faced by the Superintendents during my tenure as Assistant Superintendent in Jackson. I was aware of the unhappiness, anger, fear and problems of many parents as well as students. I had noted incidents in classrooms and on school campuses, but much of my information came from the media. In my position, I didn't have to deal with these problems except to provide training for teachers and principals who were involved. This was a far cry from having the student, parental and staff problems dumped on my lap.

What Makes the Job so Tough?

Being superintendent of schools in any large district is extremely demanding. Just the normal logistics requires an enormous amount of time, thought and energy from the top position. Managing 2,000 or more employees while keeping them motivated and attuned to the never-ending goal of improved achievement, is fraught with many sand traps. Avoiding the traps and fulfilling the vision is seldom totally achieved under the best of circumstances. Often, loud boasts are heard of enormous accomplishments from some superintendents, but most of these claims are hollow. Production is more than talk: it must be valid, proven and observable over a substantial period of time.

If managing a large school system is so difficult, imagine the added burden of running one in a swamp filled with alligators. Before you are clear of one, another is snapping at your butt. Almost all of a superintendent's time is spent fighting alligators and trying to swim to the bank instead of focusing on matters of importance for maintaining and improving the schools.

I was in a swamp. I couldn't get past one alligator until another was in hot pursuit. Not only were there groups and individuals battling to wrestle control from me, but after two or three months into the school year, there were constant and nagging problems brought to my attention daily that related to individual schools. Parents would try to get problems resolved at the school level, but the problems were so numerous that they seldom received an immediate response. So many problems were brought to the central office staff that they couldn't even reply for maybe a week or more. By that time, the major complaints had been brought to the Superintendent's office. It was obvious to me that changes that would prevent the problems from occurring were necessary, so I began to ponder the essence of the problems.

The most troubling aspect of the situation was that by the time I received a complaint, the incident or problem was usually one to two weeks old, and the person complaining had been unable to get a response from anyone in the central office chain of command. By the time it got to me, the parent was furious, and rightly so. At this point, the resolution was near impossible because of the perceived notion that no one in the schools or central office was either competent or caring. They perceived the situation they were facing as a root cause of the problems of the Jackson schools. Most of the problems were minor in nature but became monumental in the minds of those seeking solutions. I knew that something had to be done but I didn't have a ready solution.

While attending a state education conference, I met Dr. Louis Arnold, Chairman of the Department of Management at Mississippi State University. During our visit, I mentioned some of my problems to the Professor and was fascinated by his responses. When I asked if I could have an appointment in the near future to discuss the ideas further, the professor quickly agreed and a date was set.

The visit to Mississippi State University proved to be very helpful. Professor Arnold didn't attempt to provide solutions to my unique problems but instead offered applicable principles of management. One of these was "span of control" and another was the idea that "employees like a whole pie better than a slice of the pie." Both principles hit home with me because I began to see that almost all central office administrators had duties that were either district wide or involved all elementary schools or all junior and senior high schools: an unmanageable span. The Assistant Superintendent of Instruction could never spend enough time in each school to even have an inkling of what was going on throughout the district. And too, instruction was the only slice of pie the Assistant had. He had no control over other functions that enhanced his programs or rendered them ineffective. Wheels began to turn in my mind.

As I discussed this problem and the need for management change with my Advisory Committee, Hap Wilson, president of the state telephone network responded that he had on his staff one of the best management people that could be found. He offered to loan Steve Rolfe to me for a few weeks whenever I was ready to concentrate on arriving at a solution.

Reorganization for Better Management

Within two weeks, Steve reported to my office and began a study of the organizational chart and administrative personnel, along with administrator job descriptions. He then began interviewing central office and local school administrators, inquiring about functions and problems. Within three weeks, Steve Rolfe had a wealth of knowledge about the Jackson school district and its ability, or lack of ability, to function efficiently and effectively.

When Steve was ready to make his report to me, I brought in my old standbys, Dr. Joe Richardson and Dr. Jon Kinghorn, along with Dr. Tom Word, a University of Mississippi Professor, who had long tenure as a consultant to the Jackson School District, and Dr. Louis Arnold. This team, including Steve, with me participating, was charged with hearing the report and recommending a design for reorganizing the administrative team. Some of the administrators were generally thought to be tired and ineffective. However, I was convinced that they were all highly competent but had assignments that were impossible to carry out because of the magnitude of their jobs.

The team listened intently to Steve's findings. The report recommended that span of control not exceed 10 persons to manage. It also echoed the professor's comments that a one-facet assignment, when supervising schools, was neither satisfying nor effective. The study went well beyond the area of reorganization and actually pointed out major operational changes that could improve education in Jackson.

Steve's theory was that school districts are run by educators, and as such, their expertise is education, not transportation, food service, maintenance, janitorial service, etc. He pointed out that ITT made little progress in communications until it farmed out all other functions, and then concentrated on its major purpose. The team was impressed with this concept, and I knew Steve was right on target; however, this was a radical idea for public school districts, and I suggested that such a bold step be placed on the back burner and approached at a more opportune time. Right now the problem was managing the schools effectively, reducing school related problems, and bringing harmony and optimism to the community.

The designed plan involved assigning one assistant superintendent to the high schools, one to the middle schools, one to the 5th/6th grade plazas, then dividing the elementary schools into groups of 12 or 13 (which would be called areas) and assigning an assistant superintendent to each area. Al Russell would head up the high schools, moving from the personnel job, which in turn would become the responsibility of Sandra Wells. A Director of Communication with professional training had been employed earlier to assist Walter Riley, so now Walter would be assigned to oversee all middle schools, and Art Seaborne would be given full responsibility for the office of Communication. The plazas would be headed by Leon Jones, a new employee, and the elementary areas would be administered by three Area Assistant Superintendents yet to be employed. The Director of Finance would be placed directly under the Superintendent, as would be a Director of Research and Evaluation position which would be created, and then most of the subject area supervisory positions would be eliminated.

Sam Arnold, who would be retiring after one more year, would become Consultant to the person replacing him, would write a history of the Jackson Public Schools, something that had never been done. Lawson McCreary would become Assistant Superintendent for Services, replacing Sam.

Floating a Balloon

I knew better than to totally surprise the community, staff and Board so I began sending up balloons to determine which way the wind would blow on the question of reorganization. When talking with the press, I regularly referred to management problems and to the district's inability to pounce on and solve problems quickly, let alone prevent them from occurring. I emphasized how the district had grown over the years, and jobs of some central office administrators with district-wide assignments had become unmanageable. I sent a memo to board members about this deficiency and the need to reorganize in a way that would allow administrators to get a handle on their duties, prevent problems, and quickly solve those that would arise.

The central office staff and principals were aware of what was going on largely because of Steve's interviews and questions. The purpose of Steve's work was no secret to anyone. So, the only questions were about the nature of changes that would take place, what new assignments would be made, and who would be affected by them.

Board Approves Reorganization

I was now ready to submit the plan to the Board of Education for approval. No doubt it would be approved unanimously because as Bob Ross had said when I agreed to take my position, "Be careful what you ask for because you are going to get it." There had never been a split vote on any item presented or even serious questioning of an issue during a public meeting since I had been Superintendent. So I presented the plan to the Board with a recommendation that Area Assistant Superintendent Positions be created as required by the reorganization plan.

Candidates for Area Assistants Approved

After advertising the new administrative positions, receiving applications and interviewing, I was ready to present my recommendations for approval to the Board. Although I knew that my recommendations would be accepted, I was also certain that eyebrows would be raised when I presented the candidates, in person, for the positions. No one even blinked an eye when Johnny Wise became the first black assistant superintendent in Jackson, but he was the ranking black administrator in the district. Everyone knew there would have to be some blacks in high positions. But this time it was different.

When these new Area Assistant Superintendents were recommended for approval by the Board, obvious was the fact that one was black. That was the second black assistant superintendent I had presented to the Board, and this one was an outsider. Belon Winston's eyebrows shot up and a smile quickly ensued, but that smile was singular. Nevertheless, a motion for approval was made along with a swift second by Winston, and five yeas were audible.

After the meeting, Bob Ross paced the floor while I was signing papers and attending to board related matters. When I had finished and most of the people had departed, Chairman Ross walked up to me and quietly but sternly said, "Doctor, if all my friends had been here today, I wouldn't have a damn friend in the world!" Bob Ross was as prejudiced as they came but he knew what had to be done and he had the guts to do it.

New Assistants Instructed

When the newly-appointed assistants reported for duty, and those in other assignments were moved to their new positions, I instructed the six Assistant Superintendents during their first meeting together. My instructions were: "You have an office here in the central office building, but your job is in the schools. If you spend more than 30% of your time here, you'll not be doing your job effectively. Get in the schools and be certain that a solid instructional program is available to every student. Each of you is well-trained in the level of the schools to which you have been assigned, and you are supposed to know what quality instruction is like and how to attain excellence."

"Additionally, and foremost at this point, you are to prevent problems from occurring. Don't sit around until they occur. Take preventive measures to see that there are few if any problems. Deal with problems quickly and with finesse. If school problems are brought to my office, it means you are not doing your job effectively."

"You will be responsible for all functions of your schools. Purchase orders will be approved by you, as will all major changes and directions. These are your schools, and you are responsible for seeing that they function well and meet community expectations. Get to know the people in your area, and see that the schools are friendly places, and let people know that you are there to serve them."

Within a few days after the reorganization, my phone calls, regarding school problems, diminished dramatically. Occasionally, a parent chose to skip the Principal and Assistant Superintendent and go directly to the top. I had to deal with a few, but most of the time I diplomatically referred them back to the person who had the most information about the problem and could most easily solve it. The move had been great for everyone.

Meanwhile On the Home Front

With the Viet Nam war still chugging along, more troops were needed. Our oldest son, Ricky, had just turned 19 and the draft board listed him as number 10 in the county to be called for active duty. So his time as a civilian was expected to be short.

At the end of the spring semester of his freshman year, Ricky transferred from the University of Alabama to Millsaps, a local parochial college, recognized nationally for its academic excellence. (Johnny Carson attended Millsaps College during his military service in the Jackson area.) Expecting to be called to duty at any time, Ricky wanted to be at home while awaiting his call. The call came, and as he was packing to leave, the war ended and his orders were rescinded.

Ricky finished the summer quarter at Millsaps then transferred to the University of Texas, a very expensive move. Wanda went with him to a local bank to apply for a student loan, and told him that he would have to help pay for his education.

When Rita discovered, during her junior year, that she could attend summer school and graduate from high school at the end of the summer session, Wanda and I knew we would have to squeeze our budget even tighter. We would now have two children in college during the next three years.

Modification of Plans

The plaza issue dragged on for some time after Justin Cohen and the court had agreed to renovate the Middle school to serve as the North 5th/6th Grade Plaza. The Board of Education passed a resolution asking the State Building Commission to allow the use of funds accumulated for

Jackson for the renovation project; however there was some foot-dragging. Eventually, though the project was approved and plans and specifications for renovation were finalized.

As an economic measure, the maintenance staff was assigned to do most of the work during the summer. Completion by Labor Day required that every detail that could be performed before school was out had to be done. All materials had to be lined up and ready for the opening of the plaza. There could be no delays. The staff would postpone much of the needed maintenance in other schools in order to devote maximum time to the Plaza project, but other urgent matters as well had to have attention before the summer months ended.

Work on the curriculum design was virtually complete, but there was still work to be done on aligning learning objectives and having them printed in book form. Some of the materials for teaching the objectives had been designed but more materials were needed. These would have to be printed, mostly as single sheets. This would be a monumental task for the print shop, requiring one or more additional offset presses and operators. Storage of these materials would require endless feet of shelving, which must be arranged for quick and easy retrieval of materials by both students and teachers. The cabinet shop would be hard-pressed to build these, along with cabinets required in the large open spaces created by the removal of many classroom partitions throughout the building.

A consultant who had already worked with the Jackson schools was engaged long-term to direct and oversee all things related to material development and storage. Additionally, she was assigned responsibility for training the staff to work as teams in the open spaces and assuring teacher competence in using individualized instruction as the means of teaching students.

Then there was the matter of administering the program. Who could do it? A bi-racial team was required, as it should be, but someone must be assigned to be head administrator. I, along with Leon Jones and the Consultant, decided to go with a highly regarded, long-time high school principal, and then assign assistant principals to manage specific grades and groups. Jones, being Assistant Superintendent for Plazas, took the lead in managing the entire project.

I continued to portray a countenance of calmness while the work was progressing. But beneath the façade were great doubts and fears. The Plaza idea, with large open-space classrooms, was birthed by members of the outside consulting firm. It was sold to the community as the best thing since apple pie, but was creating nervousness on the part of everyone. Adoption was made because there had to be something in the plan that could be sold to the community and the plaintiff, and would be acceptable to the court. I found it difficult to totally support this final step and to market optimism about what was being done because I had always been honest and straight-forward with the people I served. I had experienced the trauma and difficulties of team teaching earlier in my career. This may have been my most difficult moment in Jackson, but it had to be done, so we did it.

Sam Arnold was beside himself the whole summer. Summers were probably Sam's worst time of year because of the rush to get everything ready for the next school year, and this may have been the worst of all summers. But, maybe last summer was even worse with the purchase of busses and preparation for transporting pupils. Then to, there was the uncertainty of where funds would come from to cover the commitments I had made.

This summer was little different. Every time Rayburn or I would order items or ask that something special be done, as the Plaza was being prepared, Sam would return the request to me having written in the margin, "Where's the money coming from? It's not in the budget."

My stock response was, "Just do it."

Often a response would come back, "I don't know how we are going to handle it but you're the boss."

And I would return it again saying, "You got it right."

Despite the haggling, things went well at the Plaza. The maintenance crew and the cabinet makers were excellent. The work of Leon Jones, Ruth Bates and the whole crew directing and planning for the instructional program and staff training moved along well. The instructional task was so massive that from time to time Ruth threatened to quit, but I would counsel with her and send her back for more torture. Her long experience as a college professor, consultant and noted speaker enabled her to put up a good front and to motivate the staff.

The renovation project was completed sufficiently for school to begin uninterrupted. To say that things went smoothly that school year would be shading the truth, but with a few adjustments during the year, it worked.

The Other Plaza

While plans were being made to open the North Plaza, questions continued to be asked about what was being done about the South Plaza. Actually no funds could be seen forthcoming for that facility, but there was need for assurance of good faith on the part of the Board of Education. While a casual search for a site was underway, a realtor approached the Board about a substantial site in Southwest Jackson. The location seemed appropriate and the terrain acceptable. Rather than buying the land outright, the Board arranged for an option to purchase the property at an undisclosed date. This action removed the probing that had been sporadic ever since the desegregation plan was adopted, and it gave the district time to attend to other matters.

Preschool Program Funded

While in my previous position and even sometimes while superintendent, I spent time observing in first grade classrooms. The observations and analysis of available data resulted in proposed changes to the instructional program, yet I was still appalled by the results. Many teachers were still teaching every child the same thing at the same time in a classroom setting that made this approach highly inappropriate. A very high percentage of first graders were failing to learn to read by the end of their first academic year and were required to repeat the grade. This condition was devastating to youngsters, and was also uselessly costing the district large sums of money that was badly needed elsewhere.

Under my direction, a proposal for an innovative preschool program to serve economically deprived children was prepared and submitted for federal funding. This program was approved, and was housed near a federal housing project in one of the school buildings that had been closed under court order. Children attending the program were almost exclusively from families on welfare and in the vast majority of cases these were one-parent families. About 90% of the attendees were black. These children were high risk for repeating first grade because of poor reading skills.

Teachers for the program were selected carefully based on good credentials and a willingness to attend instructional training sessions and to use the methods of instruction taught by the trainers. These teachers were enthusiastic and loved children. By the end of that school year, a much higher percentage of the preschool students were reading on first grade level than were those who had just completed first grade.

On one occasion, I sat in a preschool classroom during a reading session of a group and watched the ecstatic expressions on the faces of the children, as well as their reactions, as they grasp reading concepts. Finally, the teacher, looking at the clock, said, "My goodness! We are about to miss our play time. We've been working almost an hour and must stop."

"No, no!" the children cried. "Let's keep learning!"

I was convinced as never before that the only thing poor children need in order to learn well is a competent, caring and enthusiastic teacher who will assess pre-reading and reading skills then teach that which each child is ready to learn. The same is true for learning math. More than half of teachers' time is wasted teaching children material they already know or have insufficient background for learning. Learning to teach in this manner was the essence of the staff development training that had occurred in Jackson. But many of the teachers continued to teach the same way they had taught when a large percentage of their students had similar backgrounds.

Almost all of the children who completed the preschool program were academically ready to enter first grade, with great success virtually assured. Unfortunately, funding for the program was terminated after one year. I fought with everything I had to keep this wonderful program, but it was just like the transfer of teachers in midterm, there was no winning. With Washington, you win a few and lose many. It's not what works or doesn't work; it's what some person who is lacking in knowledge, understanding, and good common sense decides. If that program could have received continuous funding and the amount doubled each year for five years, Jackson schools would have improved rapidly and dramatically in every respect.

Accreditation of Schools Major Undertaking

While I was serving as an assistant superintendent, the School board authorized the Superintendent to initiate a process of self-study of all junior high schools. This step is the first of many required for receiving accreditation by the Southern Association of Colleges and Schools. The senior high schools of Jackson had long had the SACS stamp of approval, and now steps were being taken to apply for accreditation of all junior high schools as well as elementary schools. It was said that this would be the most extensive system wide accreditation process ever undertaken nationally.

The purpose of the self-study and evaluation was to identify strengths and weaknesses and to develop a structured plan for improvement that would be monitored by SACS. The city's economic needs, as well as the necessity of offering assurance of quality to the citizens of Jackson, were instrumental in making the decision to pursue this time-consuming and arduous task at this most critical time in Jackson's history. Consultants were assigned to guide each school through the self-study and accreditation process. After approximately a year of study and compilation of extensive reports, a visiting committee would be assigned to carefully examine the reports and verify that the information was indeed accurate and then make its recommendation to SACS.

Accreditation Process Winding Down

The final step in evaluating schools for Southern Association accreditation is to have an Evaluation Committee come in to scrutinize each individual school to determine if it meets association standards as required for approval. This step was achieved in the Jackson Junior High Schools in the winter of 1972 at which time 180 consultants arrived for this arduous task. In the spring an even larger group would undertake a similar mission in the elementary schools.

Accreditation would be a crowning achievement for the Jackson District and its schools. This was another step in offering assurance that the schools were worthy of trust. All administrators of the district were looking forward to this accomplishment. Sure enough, all schools received the SACS stamp of approval. Principals received individual school certificates at SACS's annual summer conference.

Rare Commendation Received

The Visiting Committee report of one elementary school contained a special commendation of a teacher of handwriting for the outstanding work she was doing. It also commended the Principal for assigning a full-time teacher to teaching "the lost art of handwriting." Oddly, this same teacher performed so poorly in a regular classroom that almost all parents strongly objected to their child being taught by her.

The new principal while visiting classes, and this teacher's class in particular, found that her pupils had the best handwriting skills of children in any class in school. She also noted that the teacher's handwriting on the chalkboard was more nearly perfect than she had ever seen. The classroom observations resulted in that teacher being assigned to teach handwriting to all students in the school.

Educational Level 10th in Nation

Change and Challenge, the Story of Jackson, Mississippi Today was released by the Mayor's office. Quoting from the U.S. Census report, the publication said that the average Jacksonian has completed 12.1 years of school. In cities of comparable size, this was the highest general educational level in the South, and 10th highest in the entire United States. This report showed that 13.4 percent of all adults were college graduates, making Jackson the 2nd highest in the south and 8th highest in the nation. The report praised the exciting new programs and concepts of learning in its public schools. Additionally, the plaza concept and progress were also highlighted.

The report further stated that of the 1970 graduating class, 80.5% are attending junior or four-year colleges, or chose business or technical schools. Nationally, this percentage was about 60 per cent. The report further stated that a survey of the 1972 class indicated that the percentage seeking advanced training was expected to rise to 82.9. Walter Riley attributed this high percentage of graduates pursuing advanced study to the fact that Jackson schools have always provided a college-oriented curriculum and that numerous institutions of higher learning was available in Jackson and vicinity.

The National Merit Scholarship Corporation announced that 23 Jackson Public School students in the graduating class of 1972 achieved semifinalist standing in the National Merit and National Achievement Scholarship Programs. While a major, local, private school boasted of its number of Merit semifinalists, it should be noted that most of these students had been taught nine to 11 years in the Jackson Public Schools.

Enrollment Declines in Private Schools

An October, 1972, article in *The Clarion Ledger,* showed a decrease of one private school (from 27 to 26) in Hinds County, and a drop in total enrollment of 1199 or 9.3 per cent from the 1971-72 school year to the 1972-73 year.[4] Meanwhile, the Jackson school's enrollment increased .9 per cent: a rather small increase [5]but the first in a few years, and perhaps this was an indication that private schools were losing their appeal. I was encouraged by these figures. The volunteer aide program seemed to be paying dividends along with a good public relations program and other parent and community involvement practices.

Valid Evaluation Needed

Improving education programs is very difficult without first hand, valid evaluation and research data. One can surmise and project, but good data are essential for true assessment and effective planning. Far too often superintendents have skimpy data for making changes in instructional programs. I needed someone on my staff that had a strong background in research design and analysis: someone who could evaluate not only achievement, but achievement in relation to the uses and types of learning materials and methods, and how they relate to learning styles of students. I, and my instructional assistants, needed this kind of information if we were to maximize learning. I found just that person in Phillip Long, in the State Department of Education and convinced him to join the Jackson team. This was one of the best hires I made during my tenure as superintendent.

Progress not Trouble Free

While Jackson was making notable progress in bringing peace and harmony to its schools, and in restoring a degree of faith among major segments of the community, others (mostly outsiders) were constantly stirring the boiling pot. National civil rights organizations were constantly

---

4   "Private School Enrollment Registers Decline in Hinds." *The Clarion Ledger,* (October 24, 1972).

5   "Public School Figures Up." *Northside Sun,* (September 14, 1972).

agitating and demanding "more and faster." A degree of change can be tolerated, but when it becomes overwhelming, it is usually rejected in one form or the other. And that's what was causing whites to the flee public schools.

Then too, the political debates in Congress and the White House, with each party trying to position itself favorably for the next election, was causing untold damage by giving both the activists and the segregationists hope. This satanically based debate did nothing other than cause each side to harden its position.

I had been through the desegregation process elsewhere when time and patience were on my side. Instead of shoving it down the community's throat unmercifully, ideas were planted, people were assured, small change was initiated and allowed to take root, and then more changes were made. This approach caused little controversy yet met the same goal. Through this process, white students remained in the public schools. Of course Jackson's situation was entirely different because the State and the Board of Education dug in their heels and fought all the way until their backs made prints in the wall. But even here one would think that reason could prevail.

While the President was working on details of an anti-busing plan, HEW was funding black student groups to test whether their rights would be violated should they misbehave. This test involved misbehavior, so the government was, in essence, encouraging student misbehavior in order for the grantee to receive funding.

The incidents of misbehavior, walkouts and rioting gave support to the civil rights activist's contention that administrators were racially biased. For example, civil rights activists charged that the cultural differences between black and white students were not being considered in establishing expectation of behavior. It was said that black kids had not been able to get used to taking off their hats in classrooms, watching their language, not talking boisterously in the halls, and not responding to teacher demands that they say, "Yes ma'am." In other words these activist groups were saying that good behavior, manners and civility should be forgotten in public schools. In schools where that type of misbehavior was tolerated, there were few if any whites left to complain. The argument of these groups amounted to a charge that blacks were incapable of proper behavior.

I refused to give in to this kind of thinking. "Education is for everyone, black and white," I contended. "It is impossible to educate in an unruly environment, and those who cannot abide by sensible rules are not educated. Therefore, the same rules and expectations are for everyone. Otherwise there can be no equality of education."

Pressure from Parent Group

Murrah High School was said to be one of the top 10 high schools in America before desegregation occurred. The Principal chose his staff wisely and only the best teachers were retained at that school. Most of the students came from the upper economic region of Jackson. So with outstanding teachers who challenged their students with interesting lessons, there were few discipline problems at Murrah High.

When the second semester of the 1969-70 school year began, almost half of the Murrah teachers were transferred to other schools leaving it with numerous teachers the principal had not recommended or wanted. These teachers were new to Murrah High and had never taught on a level normally expected by the principal. Additionally, about 40% of the students were also unaccustomed to Murrah's demands in terms of academic climate as well as discipline standards. A school that had been one of the best now struggled to be average.

The long-time constituents of Murrah quickly became unhappy. Many of them kept their children in the school the remainder of that year, but a large number moved to all-white, private schools at the beginning of the next school year.

Before the end of the 1971-72 school year, a spokesman for the white parents made an appointment with me. Accompanied by two others, we met in my office where they laid out their complaints. Knowing that the teachers could not be dismissed or transferred, their primary request was that the principal be dismissed because of his inability to maintain discipline in the school. While discipline problems at Murrah were significant, they probably were no worse than those of other high schools of the city. However, these parents were unaccustomed to hearing about discipline problems in their school.

While these parents had every right to be concerned, I was not about to fire the principal who had run one of the best schools in the nation until the court negated his strengths. I assured the parents that I would look into the matter and try to improve the situation, but the principal would remain at Murrah.

Racial Issues Flair

Racist literature outlining ways of getting black students expelled was dumped on several campuses, allegedly by passersby. The tracts were picked up by students and teachers. When I was alerted to the incident, I called the Jackson police and the local FBI office asking them to check the matter out and to be on alert to avoid a repeat occurrence. However, this action did not discourage black activists from charging that the tract was part of a planned conspiracy to disrupt the education of black students and held white administrators accountable.

I was at the Chamber of Commerce speaking to an industrial group that was seeking a location for a new plant. While speaking, I noticed the Chamber's secretary rush into the room. As I finished my presentation, the secretary moved quickly to my side handing me a note which said, "Call your office immediately. There is a major problem."

I accompanied the secretary as she directed me into a private office with a phone. As soon as I dialed the number, Beth Noles answered. "You've got to get here quickly," she said nervously.

"What's wrong?" I asked.

"There's a group of blacks holding a news conference on the front steps here, and you need to get here quickly," she demanded.

"What are they discussing?" I wanted to know.

"They're claiming that we are discriminating against black students by expelling more of them than white students," she explained.

Everything's alright. Just relax and be calm and I'll be there after a while," I assured her.

"No, you need to be here now," Beth pleaded.

"Just be calm, and call me back here when they are all gone. If I were there now, I'd have no facts for answering their charges. I'll have my own news conference tomorrow when I'll have information for responding."

Upon arriving at my office, I directed Beth and Sue Ann to call all principals and have them submit a report of all expulsions and suspensions, by race, which had occurred during the past 12 months. The figures were to be in my hands by 9:00 a.m. the following morning.

These charges had been made even though those making them were well-educated people who were knowledgeable of all civil rights activities and studies. Only seven months earlier a combination of national civil rights organizations had widely distributed reports of their scrutiny of southern schools in which they charged that the districts were using expulsion and suspension of black pupils to thwart meaningful desegregation. The groups singled out four districts that included Jackson, where it was said that forceful leadership had resulted in significant progress in working towards equal education.

When questioned by the local press about the charges, the spokesman for the group admitted that he had no numbers, but assured the press that expulsions had increased. It seemed to me that black activists were constantly searching for any excuse they could scratch up to stir the race issue. This constant harassment of school officials was one of the more damaging elements in my efforts to build a fine unitary school system.

No one could have been more surprised than I when figures from the Principal's reports had been compiled. Only three expulsions had taken place over the past year. Two of these were black and one white. The suspension data were entirely different. There had been large numbers suspended, with figures that would have been somewhat supportive of the black's complaint had they concentrated on suspensions rather than expulsions. But they didn't.

I called a news conference during which I blasted the charges, presented the numbers, and stated that I was shocked that only three students had been expelled in the past 12 months. I questioned whether disciplinary measures had been sufficiently severe, and I assured the community that Principals would be asked to strictly enforce discipline and apply appropriate measures.

That was the end of news conferences at the central office, called by black activists wishing to condemn school officials.

Near Collapse of High School Building

An announcement of plans for a large, new downtown Holiday Inn hotel was a positive sign for a city that had been shunned for other potential capital projects within the past few years. Articles in local newspapers said the hotel, including a large parking deck, would be built adjacent to Central High School.

The owner and the contractor came to my office and explained the construction plans and procedures, and how they would excavate within a few feet of the school for the foundation and part of the first level of the parking deck. They discussed the projected noise level and their plans for keeping it to a minimum. A written agreement was presented, containing a hold-harmless clause, which I was asked to sign. The first thought that crossed my mind was that any action on my part that would prevent, or even delay, construction of the hotel would not be received with enthusiasm by the city, the Chamber of Commerce or the community. However, I didn't want to sign the agreement without approval of the school board attorney and the Board. I assured the Holiday Inn officials that I would secure action on the matter quickly. Both the attorney and the Board were quick to give approval to the request. I returned the signed document to the requesting authority.

A few weeks later, the Central High principal called to tell me that the construction project was endangering the safety of his building. Shortly after that call, I also received a call from the construction superintendent asking me to come to the site to observe the problem. Extensive efforts had already been made, with little success, in stopping the soil that was moving from underneath the high school. Large pilings driven into the ground had broken from the pressure as if they were toothpicks.

The owner and contractor were unaware of soil conditions in that area. Yazoo clay is common in the Jackson area. This clay is found in much of the rolling areas of the city and surrounding area. When it is disturbed, and sometimes when it is not, the clay starts to move and is extremely difficult to corral. At that time, no one knew why Yazoo clay behaved in this manner, but evidence of the action could be seen in broken pavement and concrete in roads, broken foundations and cracks in walls of homes, and splits in roofs of commercial buildings and schools. This is something that has caused untold problems and expense in the Jackson area.

Yazoo clay was oozing from underneath Central High School and panic was in the air. A solution had to be found quickly, or at least that end of the school building would collapse. After extensive consultation with engineers and others familiar with the construction problems in the area, A solution was found, and the hotel and the parking deck were completed.

City Schools Must Fire 400 Employees

I released a statement to the staff and media in which I noted that the Jackson Public School System was contemplating a major reduction in federally funded programs and services for the 1973-74 school year.

At a press conference, I said, "Barring unforeseen developments, this cutback stands to eliminate as many as 400 teaching, administrative, clerical and teacher aide position now existing under the federally funded Title I and Title IV-A programs. As part of this effort, our plans call for a major reduction in our central office work force."

The proposed cutback further called for the phasing out of the three child development centers which became operational in Jackson the previous summer under the Title IV-A program. "The handicapped children's services center at Watkins school will continue to operate, but with a reduced staff," I stated. I explained that the cutback was being necessitated by recent national developments affecting federal aid to education. "In view of these events, we can no longer offer assurances to federally funded employees that they will be rehired in their present positions next year," I added. I further stated that the situation could change at any time and I hoped it would, but plans would have to be made for the next school year on the basis of the information available now.

"I would like to point out that insofar as we have been able to identify them, the persons who are likely to be affected by the cutback have been apprised of the situation as it now stands," I said. "The decision to reduce services and personnel was not easy to make, but the only other alternative available is to seek a tax increase to continue to support the programs as they now exist," I explained. "In view of the current tight money situation, both locally and nationally, we feel that a tax increase cannot be justified just now. We have no other choice but to tighten our belts, so to speak. The cutback in services and personnel will mean a savings of approximately $800,000 for the school district," I told them. I pointed out that the services scheduled to be terminated are programs that were designed to provide special help above and beyond the regular instructional program, and that they have done this. "While these services, and the contributions of valued employees, will be sorely missed, I predict that the proposed cutback will have little or no adverse effect on the school system's regular instructional program," I said. "I can assure you, the Jackson Public Schools, will continue to meet the high standards set by the school system's regular instructional program." I concluded[6]

---

[6] "Must Fire 400 Employees." *The Clarion Ledger*, (March 2, 1973).

Chapter 12

Plans for Stability

I was pleased with the support I had received from both races during the past year. Certainly there had been contention from time to time, but overall I could not have, in any way, anticipated the positive relationship I had developed simultaneously with both the liberal and the conservative people of Jackson. With an increase in enrollment in the public schools and a decrease in the private school enrollment, I felt that further progress could be made, if stability could be maintained and overall program improvement could be continued on a sturdy upward course. But I could also foresee difficulties arising in the not too distant future unless plans could be devised and implemented that would assure the success of these factors.

Justin Cohen and the courts would be keeping a sharp eye on racial balance in the schools. Rapid growth of the black population, with corresponding expansion into current white neighborhoods, could be projected with certainty. Such population shifts would result in racial imbalance in schools, without constantly adjusting school boundary lines. Changing zone lines, resulting in moves to other schools would cause unhappiness of parents, pupils and teachers.

I began thinking about ways of assuring stability over a long period of time. Furthermore, I was convinced that enhanced services for adults and the business community would attract support for the schools.

Working with the district statistician, I began to visualize a plan that would encompass several large education parks, each of which would be located in a pie-shape zone extending from downtown Jackson to the outer perimeter of the city. These lines would be drawn in locations that would provide a high degree of racial balance in all the schools, yet would be permanent, regardless of population shifts. The largeness of the zones and the multiplicity of schools in each zone park would have a major stabilizing effect.

The Board of Education could purchase tracts of land near the city's perimeter each containing 100 to 200 acres. Each park would have one high school, one or two junior high schools, and approximately four elementary schools. Each school site could serve as a community education and recreation center where some parts of the buildings, such as libraries, gymnasiums and classrooms, as well as outdoor facilities staffed by the city recreation department, would be available to the people in that zone. Police and fire department substations could be built on each site, helping to assure security of facilities and safety of participants.

This was a dream that would require much thought, a major selling job, and extensive cooperation never before witnessed in Jackson. First, the School Board would have to embrace the concept. Justin Cohen and Fred Ware would have to ensure their support. Then the Mayor and City Council would have to buy into this elaborate and costly plan and agree to provide substantial funding for each project or site. The federal court would have to approve the plan. And finally, the concept would have to be sold to the citizens of Jackson. The plan would be long-range, requiring development of each education park on an as-needed basis, taking perhaps as long as 20 years to complete. Financing would include funds from the sale of unneeded schools and unused lands as parks were developed.

As soon as I was convinced that my dream was worth pursuing, I began reducing it to written form, with more details that could be shared with others. First, I sent a copy to Bob Ross and Henry Long, "for your review and discussion." We three met, had a brief discussion and the plan received a firm endorsement. In fact, Henry suggested that the Board select a real estate appraiser and begin appraising selected properties immediately.

Every major change I had made since becoming superintendent had received the approval of two people prior to implementation: Justin Cohen and Fred Ware. If either had known I had consulted the other, the plans would not have been accepted. But with approval of both, there was always adequate support. Each man represented the peak of the power structure of his respective group—liberal or conservative. Their approval then would trickle down through the levels of the power structure to their entire constituents. Their endorsement meant there would be little or no vocal opposition.

I made appointments with each of these gentlemen to discuss my park idea, which I believed would result in stabilizing the schools and in garnering community support for the public schools. As usual, each, with some hesitation, agreed to provide support. I met with Mayor Richard Miles and briefed him on the concept and told him that Ross and Long, as well as Cohen and Ware had endorsed the park idea. Mayor Miles appeared enthusiastic and assured me that a majority of the Council would support the plan. A copy of the concept was now mailed to each Board member, "For your perusal and perhaps later consideration."

Superintendent's Stock Rising

I was surprised when I received a call from Dr. Truman Pierce, Dean of Education at Auburn University. Dean Pierce chatted briefly then posed the question, "Would you be interested in being Superintendent of the Birmingham City Schools?"

I hesitated before responding. "Things here are moving in a positive direction," I stated before being interrupted by the Dean.

"Yes, I'm very aware of that, and so is the Board I am working with."

"We have lots of plans which are pretty exciting, and the staff has come together as a team! The family is rather contented here now. I don't know how to respond to your question."

Dean Pierce said with assurance, "The job is yours if you want it. All you have to do is say yes."

During the conversation, I was recalling my experiences as a consultant in that district while I worked in the desegregation center at Auburn. The staff was almost totally inbred. They could scarcely think beyond the limits of the city. My efforts to provide the help they needed to overcome many of their problems relating to desegregation were thwarted. Most of the top staff were within five to 10 years of retirement and were not interested in breaking the mold. While some were capable of performing well, others were rather incompetent. I had faced such a staff in Jackson and my interest in starting over wasn't compelling.

"Dean, I've started many things here that I desperately need to follow up on. I have great support from the Board and the community. I feel like I need to stay here."

"I understand," the Dean responded.

"I appreciate the offer, and especially with it being delivered by you," I said.

Observing an Education Park

Now I was ready for the next step in developing my plan. I wanted to take a select group to Pontiac, Michigan to view the park they had developed. Seeing the real thing in action enhances the sale of an idea. So, to make the trip I invited Mayor Richard Miles, with Henry Long representing the Board, and four other influential members of the community. We flew into Detroit, rented a van and drove to Pontiac where we were greeted by the Superintendent of Schools and given a briefing of the park, its contents and purpose, and how it functioned. The group was escorted on a tour of the park, and then met with some community members who were being served by the facilities. We were free to examine the facilities and talk with staff. Although the Pontiac Park was more limited than those planned for Jackson, it provided a revealing overview of what "could be" at home. Those making the trip obviously were impressed with that which they had viewed in the Pontiac School District and were eager for progress to be made in Jackson.

A Broader Plan Envisioned

The plans I was pursuing were not limited to the parks. I wanted to look at boarder needs in terms of all facilities that would enhance the operation of the district, and provide better education. Also they must garner community support for the schools, and hopefully attract more white students away from private schools.

Vocational Education

The court had ordered that vocational education for the district be housed at Northwest High, a school located in a major ghetto area where few white people would go. Almost all whites immediately withdrew from the program. The quality deteriorated quickly. I talked with business people about the competence of its graduates along with other aspects of the program and found the condition to be deplorable. A black man who owned a major construction firm was included in the discussion. He was quick to say that the program should be closed. He said he would rather hire a person with good academic skills and train him or her than to employ a graduate of the program who supposedly was already trained. That was the consensus of the group.

I envisioned a totally new, large vocational facility that would serve students from all high schools during the day and other students and adults at night. Any time an adequate number of people wanted to participate in a certain program, it would be provided at night. This service would encourage adults to upgrade skills, prepare for a different trade, or to further develop their hobbies. Additionally, the facilities could provide training for employees of any existing business or industry and for "startup" companies coming to Jackson, or to the state.

I wanted to talk with the industrial development boards, as well as with Governor William Waller, who recently had replaced Governor John Bell Williams, about offering this service to surrounding areas for a fee. Readymade vocational training, available to businesses and industries looking for a site would be an added incentive for them to locate in Jackson, or in the state of Mississippi. The vocational education facility would need adequate land in order to add state funded facilities which would be required for this unique industrial "startup" training.

Community Education

For a number of years the Jackson School District had provided community education opportunities on a limited scale with rather limited participation. Encouraged by the participation and effectiveness of the volunteer teacher substitute venture, I was certain that greater support for the public schools could be gained through a community education program that appealed to a large percentage of the citizens of all ages. I was also certain that those directly involved in the schools would know more about them and be more positive toward public education.

Currently, courses such as sewing, cake decorating, bridge, and GED preparation were available. Other courses could be added if there were qualified teachers and enough students to pay the salaries. I was thinking in terms of serving several thousand adults.

If I could get the courts to allow vocational education facilities to be constructed on a neutral site, it could serve high school students during school hours and then serve community education enrollees during all other hours. Even high school students could participate in an evening course. And out of district people could enroll when adequate space was available. This would be a great opportunity for people in the Jackson area to learn a new trade or to upgrade their skills and income. Additionally, such a program would give the Jackson area a pool of skilled workers: a great drawing card for new industries and businesses.

The volunteer program would be another component of community education. Volunteers could serve as aides in classrooms, libraries, on playgrounds and in physical education classes. They could work as tutors at all levels, and could read stories to the younger children. Volunteers could assist in special activities in schools. They could help with loading busses, directing crossing guards, and assist in after school child care. Parents who serve at their child's school would find that their child's performance would improve and their own attitude toward teachers and the school would do likewise. These experiences would cause them to reinforce their child's education greatly.

A training program would become a vital part of screening and training volunteers. The community education staff would be responsible for recruiting, screening and orientation, or training, of volunteers. This process would prevent having volunteers in schools who would be of little value, or even be disruptive.

The community education program would be largely self-supporting through fees paid by students to cover the cost of teachers and materials. Additionally, vocational education and community education funds from state and federal programs could cover other expenses. These programs would be instrumental in providing increased stability, and could possibly attract more white students to the Jackson schools.

Central Office Needs

Space was a premium in the central office. A former elementary school had been converted for offices, and as the district grew in size, and numerous new state and federal programs came into existence, the staff mushroomed greatly. This growth created a shortage of space resulting in housing staff and functions in buildings scattered throughout the city. With the staff so widespread, supervision became difficult. I found it impossible to monitor and properly guide the outsourced programs and personnel sufficiently to assure proper direction and quality.

Since I was responsible for the overall operation of the entire district I needed to consolidate the staff into a single facility so that each division, department and function could receive adequate attention and supervision. I reluctantly decided to include a new central office and related facilities in my plan for improving education in Jackson.

Search for Park Sites

When time would allow, I began driving around the perimeter of Jackson looking for sites that might be suitable for education park locations. These would need to be distributed in such a way that attendance zone lines could be drawn to include an acceptable ratio of black and white pupils in each. I was hoping I could find at least six suitable pieces of property containing 150 to 200 acres on which the Board of Education could obtain an option to purchase. Of course, the Board had not yet approved my proposed long-range plan.

One Saturday afternoon as I was surveying the city for park locations, I happened upon a large tract of land on the northwestern side of the city which attracted my attention. The land was clear of most trees, and much of it had been used extensively for some unknown purpose. "This would be an excellent site for a park," I thought. After some research, I found that the land belonged to the federal government and had formerly been a waterways experiment station site. Obviously the site had been abandoned several years. My curiosity led me to do further research of the property, and to my amazement, the government had declared the land surplus, and it was available to governmental entities, free of charge, upon submission of an approved application. Before I went too far, I decided to submit my long-range plan to the Board. If there was sufficient interest in the plan, then I would ask for permission to submit an application for the waterworks land.

Long-Range plan offered Board

I prepared a detailed long-range plan for facility development which included education parks, community education, vocational education, central office needs, and the waterworks property. The plan included methods of financing each program and possible locations of projected facilities, as well as steps to be taken for implementation. This plan, in memo form, was sent to each board member for study and for discussion at a planned meeting the following week

Plan Approved by Board

The meeting went much better than I could have hoped. The Board was enthusiastic about the concept and directed me to move ahead immediately. Henry Long again suggested that a land appraiser be selected and begin appraising some of the school district's property as discussed in the report. They also approved the submission of an application for the waterworks property, which was prepared quickly by the staff and submitted to HEW.

Plan for Selling Concept to Community

I had already considered the necessity of the community buying into the Board's long range plan for the education parks and for totally revising the attendance zones. I had thrown out ideas about the plan in news releases as a means of planting seeds. Now the emerging plans needed plenty of TLC.

While I had said that I would never participate in a question and answer program aired to the community, I changed my mind. I met with Fred Ware, who had brokered the desegregation plan with the Board, and was owner, or part-owner, of a local TV station. I discussed my idea of having a weekly "Ask the Superintendent" program, whereby I would discuss the park concept and solicit questions from the audience. I was certain the community would endorse the idea if they had all of the information about it, and had all of their questions answered in an open and honest way. The question: would the TV station be interested in airing such a program? Mr. Ware, for a change, was excited about doing this type of community service program. He assured me that he would arrange with the station manager and programming staff for details to be worked out as soon as I was ready. "They'll be ready when you're ready." Ware assured me.

Chapter 13

Offer Too Good to Refuse

I received a call from Dr. Cecil Tucker, a professor at the University of South Carolina, asking if I would be interested in the Superintendency in that state's capital city. I responded that I would not. The professor called back the next day and told me that the School Board was highly interested in talking with me. Again, I told the professor that I was happy in Jackson and planned to stay. A few days later I received a third call saying the Board had conducted a nationwide search and had turned down all applicants. "They want you as their superintendent," the professor said. Again, I turned down the job and told the professor that I intended to stay in Jackson. I also told him that my wife and I were leaving for a three-week vacation.

"The Board needs to have a superintendent employed before we return, so don't call me again."

Wanda and I had a great and refreshing vacation while my mother stayed with the children. The first day back in office, I had another call from the professor. "I asked you not to call me again," I stated firmly. "I'm tired of these calls, and I don't want another one."

The next day I received still another call. I revealed my irritation with the caller then said, "I can think of nothing that would make me leave Jackson," then hesitating, "except money." Quickly, I said, "Forgive me. I've never said anything like that before in my life. I don't know what made me say such a thing."

The professor quickly asked, "How much money?"

"I don't know," I responded.

"Well just give me a figure," he said.

After a few seconds, I said, "Fifty thousand and all relocation expense and a car."

"I'll call you right back," came his response.

Within the hour the return call came. "The money seems to be OK and the board wants to talk with you. Do you want to come here, or would you rather they come to Jackson?" he asked.

"They will learn more about me if they come here," I told him.

"Then some of the Board members will be there tomorrow," the professor assured me.

At home that evening, Wanda and I talked at length about the possible move. I told her that I had received tremendous satisfaction from that which I had been able to accomplish in Jackson, but, "I have to kick myself out of bed each morning to go to work. Prior to Jackson I always enjoyed my work and looked forward to Mondays and mornings. With two children in college, we need money more right now than we will ever need it. Let's consider this job offer. If we reach an agreement to go to Columbia, and if things go well, we'll stay there. If they don't, then I want to find a job in a small school district and enjoy the remainder of my career."

"Well, going from $33,000 to $50,000 should make life easier," concluded Wanda.

With that said, all agreed to accept the offer if the details could be worked out to our satisfaction. While unhappy with the idea of moving from Jackson and leaving Rita behind to attend Milsaps College, there was also an air of excitement about a possible change of scenery.

Before departing Jackson, late that afternoon, the three visiting Board members came back to my office to tell me that the offer still stood. "However, we can't pay you $50,000 because that's what the Governor makes, but we will pay you $49,900 and give you enough benefits that you will receive more than 50. We will also pay your real estate fee both when you sell and when you purchase a new home. And when you buy your new home, we will get you a special interest rate. We will also pay for an interior decorator and for the expenses of decorating. Now we want you and your wife to spend this weekend with us, arriving on Friday evening and returning home on Sunday. We want you to meet with some of the local people on Saturday."

Now Most Dreaded Part

I dreaded having to talk with my great boss, Bob Ross, but the next morning I went by to see him. Bob had already gotten wind of the possibility of a move from people the visiting board had talked with.

"Yeah, I know what you want to talk about, so come on in," Ross said.

"Mr. Ross, I really don't want to leave Jackson, but I've received an offer of $50,000 plus to move. We have two kids in college, which is draining us financially. I know that Jackson cannot suddenly give me anything close to that figure. My wife and I have been invited to visit with the Board and tour the city this weekend, and if we like what we see and can work out the details, I think it would be in our best interest to move," I concluded.

Ross slowly raised his large frame from his chair, characteristically paced the floor, then suddenly faced me and said, "I've worked with four superintendents, and I want you to know, I'd rather work with you than with any of the others, and if you leave, I'll resign from the Board."

"Then I'm staying in Jackson," I replied.

"No, you go on. Brandon Sparkman has to look out for Brandon Sparkman because no one else is going to do that," retorted Ross. "If this is best for you, then you need to go."

I said, "I can't leave if you are going to resign. My being here is rather unimportant. You can employ a good superintendent who, with the help of our staff, can carry on much of what we have started. But, you are the most important person in building a quality school system. If you resign, the district will fall apart. So, if you're leaving, I'm staying".

"Alright," said Ross, "I'll stay on, but you'll have to help me."

"I'll do anything I can," I replied. "What can I do?"

"When we had our last vacancy, we employed this important professor out of Georgia to conduct a nationwide search for a superintendent. We agreed to pay him a handsome sum, but almost as soon as he signed the contract, he left the country and didn't return until we had hired you. He arranged with a sidekick to help him with the search, but it was left up to him to handle the whole job. I don't want to go through that again. You know administrators all over the country, and I want you to search out three or four good ones for us to interview."

"Are you sure you want me to do this?" I inquired.

"Listen, I trust your judgment on this more than anyone I know, so that's what I want you to do if you decide to leave," Ross replied. "Now, assure me of one other thing. If you are leaving, I want you to continue on this job, either full-or part-time until we get a new superintendent on board. I don't want an interim superintendent."

"That's fine with me. I'm sure we can work that out."

Positive Greeting

Wanda and I were greeted warmly by two board members at the airport in Columbia. We were driven to the city's best hotel and told that arrangements had been made for us to order anything we wanted and to charge it to the room.

I was informed that I would be picked up at 9:45 a.m. and be escorted to a meeting with some of the influential people of the city and county. I would meet the other board members there; be introduced to the invitees; have refreshments; and after an introductory statement by the Board Chairman, would be asked to make some comments to the gathering.

After the 10 o'clock meeting there was scarcely a spare moment as we were escorted around town, dined, questioned and introduced. Late Saturday afternoon the Board members and I had a short meeting to ask and answer questions. They insisted that I begin my duties there on the first of the next month, which was slightly less than a week away. I told them of my agreement with the Jackson Board, and they relented with me working half-time in each district with the new Board giving me a full salary, and travel expenses between districts. With that agreement, the next morning, Wanda and I headed back to Jackson where I informed Bob Ross of my decision and the agreement we had made.

Counter Offer

Monday afternoon, I received a call from Mayor Richard Miles. "I hear that you have accepted a job in another city?" the Mayor inquired.

I told him that I had a difficult time deciding to leave Jackson and thanked him for his support since coming to the city.

"Well, we don't want you to leave. As a matter of fact, the city is prepared to pay you the difference between your current salary and what you'll make in the new position if you'll stay here," the Mayor urged.

Making another difficult decision, I said, "Mayor, I desperately want to say 'Yes' to you, but I can't. You see, I have given my word to the new Board that I will take the job. Furthermore, you can't have two masters. I know that I could work well with you and the current Council, but if a new mayor is elected sometime, I can't be sure of the compatibility of that new relationship. If I take pay from two sources, I have an obligation to answer to both and that could get sticky quickly,"

"I understand, but we hate to see you go. You've done a tremendous job here, and I wish you well."

Preparing for Changeover

I decided that I would spend Monday, Tuesday and Wednesday in Jackson and Thursday, Friday and Saturday on the new job. This worked rather well, but was a major overload.

I started the superintendent search immediately and within three weeks I recommended three candidates for the Jackson position. After interviewing the applicants, the Board selected one and asked him to be on the job on July 1, so I served both districts approximately one month.

Waterways Land Transfer

In the meantime, the grant for the waterworks land was approved. The formal transfer of 106 acres of land on the old waterways experiment station site from the federal government to the Jackson Municipal Separate School District I labeled "the first step in the long-range plan" for the building of educational facilities in the city.

School board members, school district staff leaders, Lt. Governor William Winter, city officials and Charles Cain, Atlanta, Deputy Regional Director of the U.S. Department of Health, Education and Welfare, attended the transfer ceremony in the council chamber of City Hall.

I told the gathering that ground could possibly be broken within a few months for the construction of a fifth and sixth grade educational center on that property. "These facilities will be designed in such a way that they can house any or all elementary grades. The basis of these plans will be in keeping with the sincere hope that this school district, in years to come, may be restructured so that again you will have elementary schools, junior high schools and senior high schools throughout the district, but this time with each grouped on single sites. It is our hope and expectation that, as the city grows and expands additional buildings will be located on this 106 acre site."

I told the group that climate control, acoustical treatment, and the aesthetic beauty of the architectural design would provide an inspirational educational setting highly conducive to learning. "Furthermore, it will serve as a source of community pride." I said, "the remaining acreage on the old waterways experiment site has been divided between the City of Jackson and Mississippi College."

The long range plan, for which the south education center will be the first step, "employs the concept of large educational centers on which schools will be consolidated on tracts of 100 acres or more. The school district has applied for a planning grant to study further the possibilities of this concept".

Lt. Gov. William Winter, representing the state, said the acquisition of the land is "another step along the way in the steady progress being made in the city in general and in education in particular."

He praised the "progressive attitude" of the city schools, and said, "they are demonstrating how well they can produce educated citizens. The people of Jackson are showing how they can cope with problems and emerge a more dedicated, united people."

He stated that a strong school system would help the city keep its young people at home and help open opportunities that would enable them to stay and find as satisfying a life as they could find anywhere.

Mr. Cain commended the school district for its plans for use of the property and said he was interested in the education park concept.[7]

Schools Could Become National Model

The local newspaper asked me for an interview prior to the time I would be leaving Jackson. In my farewell interview I said that Jackson, with its many possibilities, is the most exciting place I know, and that I think the city can emerge as a national model in education if its citizens so desire.

---

[7] "Waterways Land Transfer," *The Clarion-Ledger,* (May 31, 1973).

On the subject of strengths and weaknesses of the system, I was asked what I thought were the greatest needs of the Jackson school district. I named four:

1. An improved instructional program
2. Public kindergartens.
3. A vastly expanded vocational program.
4. Long range planning of school facilities.

I said the instructional program of the Jackson Municipal Separate School District may be far above average for Mississippi, but that it is not above, or even up to, average for the nation. "It is not nearly as good as it should be," I said, "and this is where attention needs to be concentrated."

However, I stated that tremendous progress had been made in upgrading the program, and I hoped that Jacksonians would not rest until they have a program better than the national average.

I stated that I was especially pleased with the results of reading experiments in the Jackson Schools and reported that two programs in particularly have been effective. I cited working with deprived children as one, and the other, working with high achievers in the upper elementary grades.

One of the reading programs was designed by Jackson teachers, while the other was drafted by reading specialists of a publishing company. "I believe we're just on the threshold of really making great strides in instruction," I told the press. "These two programs should be placed in all elementary schools as rapidly as possible, but it will take time. The staff needs to be trained in the use of these programs, and the evaluation of the programs must be continued from year to year. About two, or more, years will be required to extend the program system-wide," I concluded.

Kindergartens Needed

"I have become convinced that kindergartens make a tremendous difference, and if I had to make a choice, I would choose kindergarten and dispense with the 12th grade. Mississippi can never expect its school children to equal those of other states in achievement unless it adds kindergarten to its public school system."

Vocational Education

I emphasized that a particularly pressing need in Jackson was an expanded and improved vocational education program. "Jackson has more problems in this area than the average Mississippi school district, yet all share the same problem: the stigma attached to vocational education by parents of some children. It is not for low achievers, for both low and high achievers can excel in it," I projected. "I have had no difficulty finding agreement among parents about the need for vocational training, but what they also agree on is that it's for somebody else's child. But, that's where the money is. There's a crying need for vocational skills now, and the need will become greater," I said.

I pointed out that Jackson has the additional problem of having its vocational program locked in by court order to a virtually all black school in a declining neighborhood. I stated that although agreement between the plaintiffs and the defendant school district in the Jackson school desegregation case could probably produce a change, the parties have not yet been able to put an agreement together.

"Funds are available through the state and federal governments for building a vocational technical center, but school leaders fear they will never be able to achieve a workable program at its present location. And without concentrating the training in a new, better equipped center, located in a racially neutral zone, there is little hope for improvement," I told the press.

I pointed out that the school district owns a tract of land north of Lake Hico, near the future route of Interstate 220, that is being considered as a site. Several representatives of the black community are known to be agreeable to this plan, and continued effort needs be exerted to hurdle this obstacle.

School Locations

"I believe a long range planning program is necessary to provide adequate physical facilities in places where they will be needed. The location of the South Jackson Educational Center on the old waterways experiment station site is perhaps the first step in this direction."

I said that Jackson has some great strength in its system that will bolster it in meeting these various needs. One of these is the support of the city's civic and business leadership. "Because of this, we have made progress," I said, "and if it were withdrawn, the school system would be hurt badly."

"I think the races have tried very hard to work together. Racial attitudes are not what they should be but, by and large, there has been very good cooperation. I have no more of an answer for racial prejudice than anybody else, but I do suggest people are going to have to put their reputation on the line and say what they ought to say and do what they ought to do for the good of the community."

Good Organization

"Strength of the Jackson City Schools," I said, "is a well-organized central office staff. We have reorganized the staff during my tenure here as superintendent, and the organization is working exceedingly well. I think that while the new superintendent is coming in and 'getting his feet on the ground,' the present staff can maintain the momentum and perform effectively. Jackson has a good instructional staff, but there must be constant work to upgrade it."[8]

A Parting Surprise

I received letters, notes and phone calls from staff and citizens of the community thanking me and lamenting my departure. But the one letter that surprised and pleased me most was from former Governor, Ross Barnett, a person elected governor because of his fierce opposition to integration.

Dear Dr. Sparkman:

I was sad to learn that you will no longer be with the Jackson Public Schools. You have done an excellent job for which every Jacksonian should be grateful.

I am wishing you much success.

Very sincerely yours,
Ross R. Barnett

---

[8] "Sparkman says Local Schools Could Become National Model," *The Clarion-Ledger, Ledger,* (June 1, 1973).

Epilogue

After two years in Richland District I, Columbia, South Carolina, I decided to leave and look for a small school district where I could enjoy the remainder of my career. I returned to my native state of Alabama where I served my final years as superintendent of schools in the beautiful town of Guntersville.

I made no effort to keep track of what was transpiring in Jackson after I left there. However, I know that the concept of developing education parks was dropped. Years later I learned that the schools of Jackson had arrived at virtually the same place of many intercity schools—almost as segregated as it was in 1954 when the *Brown vs. Board of Education* decision was handed down by the U.S. Supreme Court.

I retired from education in 1988, and then established an education publishing and consulting firm which took me to many parts of America. I sold the company a few years later, and afterward, taught graduate courses for the University of Alabama, Birmingham, as an adjunct professor.

Currently, my wife, Anne, and I reside at our lake home in Muscle Shoals, Alabama, where I am semi-retired and pursuing my lifelong hobby of writing.

References

Jackson Daily News
The Clarion-Ledger
Northside Sun
Boca Raton News
Saturday Review
Education Taskforce, Jackson Chamber of Commerce